WHISKY
Talk

WHISKY
Talk

A SPIRITED COLLECTION

OF FACTS AND

ESSENTIAL INFORMATION

ON THE WHISKIES

OF THE WORLD

ANDREW JONES

PIATKUS

© 1997 Andrew Jones

First published in Great Britain by
Judy Piatkus (Publishers) Ltd
5 Windmill Street, London W1P 1HF

The moral right of the author has been asserted

A catalogue record for this book is
available from the British Library

Designed by Suzanne Perkins/Grafica
Illustrations by Madeleine David

ISBN 0–7499–1755–5

Set in 11/14 pt Frutiger Light by
Intype London Ltd, London SW19
Printed and bound in Great Britain by
Mackays of Chatham plc, Chatham, Kent

Contents

Preface

I really hope that reading this book will be as much fun as writing it was. The same can't be said of the research, during which seven fractures of the left wrist were sustained without having touched a single drop of the golden liquor. However, the good fortune of being right-handed permitted *Whisky Talk* to be completed on time – though medication reduced liquid intake for a while.

The book is intended to amuse, entertain and enlighten with its facts, legends, anecdotes and stories from the whiskies of the world, gathered in two decades of drinks journalism. I do not pretend to be a great whisky-taster, but one with an enthusiasm for the history and background of the subject and a fascination with its multitude of styles.

While I have made every effort to check, re-check and constantly update the information in the book, inevitably some of it may be superseded by the time it reaches the shelves. However, be assured that the facts are true and correct to the best of my knowledge at the time of publication.

Extremes

Christmas Day whisky One of the most unusual whiskies must be Glengoyne 1967, which was distilled on Christmas Day and produced just 2500 bottles. Other limited vintage bottlings were made for 1968, '69 and '70; only 1200 bottles are available from '70 and it is forecast that a mere 1000 from 1971 will follow. However, the 'three wise men' of Glengoyne – the manager, mashman and stillman – could never be persuaded to work on Christmas Day again.

coldest water source Dorie's Well, the source for the Singleton of Auchroisk, is reputed to be the coldest in Scotland at 7.6°C (45.50°F).

double malt Robert, the bartender in the record-breaking malt whisky bar at the Ritz-Carlton in San Francisco, reports that he is occasionally asked for a 'double malt' by those who have only just heard of a single malt and who naively believe a double one will be superior. He has to exercise supreme tact in his response to ensure the customer is not embarrassed.

highest priced bottle of whisky ever A 50-year-old Glenfiddich fetched the equivalent of £49,604 at a charity auction in Milan in December 1992.

highest priced Scotch single malt listed In January 1997 the Bowmore distillery on the island of Islay listed 294 bottles of a unique 40-year-old 1955 Bowmore single malt at £4500 each. In total, 306 bottles were filled from one unique hogshead with an overall value of

£1,323,000 ($2,182,950). Two bottles were placed in the distillery's museum and ten have been securely locked away. The £4500 includes overnight hospitality, a tour of the distillery and a complimentary dram from one of those ten bottles.

In 1955 an anonymous private customer had ordered the distillery to fill an oloroso-sherry butt and age the whisky for 20 years, then advise him when it would be ready for collection. The butt sprang a leak and about 20 per cent of the whisky was lost, in addition to the normal evaporation of about 40 per cent. Subsequently, the distillery manager decanted the remaining contents from the butt (500 litres, 132 US gallons) into a once-used Kentucky Bourbon hogshead (250 litres, 66 US gallons) and tried to contact the customer, only to learn that he had just died. Bowmore purchased the whisky from his estate and aged it for another 20 years.

largest pot still in Europe   The Midleton distillery near Cork, Ireland, had an early nineteenth-century still with a capacity of 143,874 litres (37,977 US gallons) which was in use until 1975.

largest malt whisky distillery   The Tomatin distillery in the Monandiiath mountains 14 miles (22.5 kilometres) south of Inverness in the Highland region of Scotland, has 23 pot stills with a combined capacity of 368,000 litres (97,218 US gallons). It has 16 warehouses with sufficient space for 230,000 filled casks.

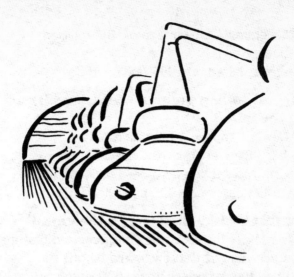

largest selling whiskies in the world
1 Johnnie Walker Red: approx. 91 million bottles
2 J & B Rare: approx. 72 million bottles
3 Jim Beam: approx. 67 million bottles
(Statistics based on 1996 published figures)

largest selling premium Scotch whiskies in the world
1 Johnnie Walker Red: approx. 91 million bottles
2 J & B Rare: approx. 72 million bottles
3 Ballantines: approx. 59 million bottles
(Statistics based on 1996 published figures)

largest selling premium whisky in the
UK Bell's Extra Special, an eight-years-old blended Scotch whisky. Its 1995 sales represented approximately 18.7 million bottles.

largest selling premium whiskies in the USA
1 Jim Beam: approx. 45.2 million bottles
2 Jack Daniel's: approx. 36 million bottles

3 Seagrams 7 Crown: approx. 35.9 million
  bottles
(Statistics based on 1995 published figures)

largest selling premium Scotch whiskies in the USA

1 Dewars: approx. 18.2 million bottles
2 J & B Rare: approx. 10.1 million bottles
3 Clan McGregor: approx. 9.3 million bottles
(Statistics based on 1995 published figures)

largest whisky distillery in the world

On 5 May 1937 the *Louisville Times* reported that the Seagram-Calvert distillery would be officially opened the next day with 10,000 visitors expected to attend the ceremony and look over 'the world's largest distillery'. Its capacity was stated to be 10,000 bushels of grain a day, producing 189,265 litres (50,000 US gallons) of whisky every 24 hours. It would employ 1800 people (a figure which may have been exaggerated) and its warehouses could hold 85,283,034 litres (22,530,000 US gallons) or 450,720 barrels.

longest continuous ownership of any distillery

This is believed to be that of the Springbank distillery, Campbeltown, Scotland, acquired by John and William Mitchell in 1837. It was previously owned by their in-laws, called Reid. Today the family company remains in control under the sixth generation of Mitchells.

longest serving distillery employee

George Ross, 1873–1958, worked at the Glenmorangie distillery in Tain, Scotland, from 1886 to 1958, a remarkable 72-year span which covered six British monarchs. When he started in the distillery's private piggery at the age of 13 the car had not yet been invented. By 1895 he had become a stillman and held that role during the First World War and the Second World War, when he was one of only three staff. He ended his career in the cooperage, when the exploration of space was well under way.

longest serving distillery manager   Another record is claimed by Glenmorangie with Gordon Smart, who led the distillery team known as 'the sixteen men of Tain' for 49 consecutive years from 1921 to 1970. Before that he was manager for couple of years until 1910.

most visited Scotch whisky distillery   Glenturret in Crieff, Perthshire, received a record 228,416 visitors in 1996.

most visited whisky distillery in the world   The Jack Daniel's distillery at Lynchburg, Tennessee, USA, holds the annual record with a total of 314,482 visitors in 1982, and provides the most charming and relaxed visit.

oldest surviving whiskey distillery in the world   The title is claimed by The Old Bushmills distillery in County Antrim, Northern Ireland, with a licence dating from 1608 which was granted to Sir Thomas Phillipps.

only kosher Bourbon in the world   Old Willamsburg is certified by a Jewish organisation known as Hisachdus Harabonim.

only triple-distilled Scotch single malt   Auchentoshan, a delightfully elegant and particularly fine malt, is one of the lightest because it is the only Scotch single malt that is triple-distilled. This is the last vestige of a practice called *trestarig*, begun generations before 1823 (Auchentoshan's foundation date) by Irish monks who settled the area. Unfortunately, inaccurate assumptions have been made that certain other whiskies are triple-distilled.

smallest distillery in Scotland   The Edradour at Balnauld, near Pitlochry in the Highland region, is operated by just three men. Its annual output is the equivalent of one week's production at an average-sized distillery. Its spirit-still holds only 2182 litres (8,259 US gallons) and only 24,000 bottles are made available for retail sales each year.

tallest pot stills in Scotland   The record is claimed by Glenmorangie, with stills at 16 feet 10¼ inches (5.1 metres). Taller stills produce lighter more elegant malts while short, stubby ones provide fuller flavours.

The ultimate blend   In 1995 Justerini & Brooks achieved a great coup when they launched Ultima, a blend of 128 different malt and grain whiskies. The company said that they had included whiskies from 96 of the 98 distilleries in Scotland; the two that were excluded, Kininvie and Speyside, were too young for their needs at just three years. Among the most treasured constituents were casks of Milburn, long since closed and converted to a Beefeater chain restaurant, and Glen Mhor, which was bulldozed out of existence in 1983. J & B were only able to acquire single casks of some malts and Ultima is therefore strictly limited, as the numbered bottles imply. Stocks will probably be exhausted around the year 2002. As a result, bottles numbered under 1000 are becoming valuable collector's items.

the ultimate tax   In 1996 The Scotch Whisky Association estimated that the combined annual taxation bill paid by the Scotch whisky distillers was just over £1 billion ($1.6 billion).

first recorded distillery in Scotland   Ferintosh, near Culloden in the Highland region, was clearly founded before 1689. Owned by Duncan Forbes, a sympathiser of William of Orange, it was burned to the ground by Jacobite rivals in that year. In 1690 he was exempted from paying duty as compensation.

first licensed single malt distillery in Scotland   The Glenlivet was registered in 1824 by George Smith.

first licensed distillery in Canada   John Molson's distillery in Montreal in 1799, with the substantial capacity of 1,136,500 litres (300,239 US gallons).

first registered distillery in the USA   Jasper (Jack) Daniel of Lynchburg, Tennessee, in 1866.

first licensed distillery in Australia   Myers at Ballarat in Victoria in 1866.

first registered maltman   On 15 February 1605, Johne Wallace was registered as No. 1 entry in the Maltmen Craft in Glasgow.

first whisky advertisement   Justerini & Johnson, later Justerini & Brooks, placed an advertisement offering *Usquebaugh* and other drinks in the *Morning Post and Daily Advertiser* in London on Thursday 17 June 1779.

first commercially blended Scotch whisky   Usher's OVG (Old Vatted Glenlivet) was introduced in 1853.

first woman distiller in Scotland   Bessie Williamson held this post at Laphroaig on the island of Islay in 1946.

first purpose-built distillery in America to make whiskey   It was run by Wilhelm Hendriksen in the New Netherland territory, on what is now Staten Island, and belonged to the Dutch West India Company. It first produced spirits 'from corn and rye' in 1640.

first purpose-built commercial Kentucky distillery   Evan Williams constructed a building for distilling whiskey at the junction of Fifth and Water Streets in Ohio Falls, later Louisville, in 1783.

first Kentucky whiskey to be exported   In

1780 John Ritchie sold Kentucky whiskey in New Orleans, which was then Spanish territory.

first Kentucky Bourbon sold in bottles   Bininger's Grocers sold bottles of whiskey in New York City in 1849.

first Kentucky Bourbon sold as a brand   Old Forrester (later Forester) was produced and bottled in 1872 as a reliable, standard-quality whiskey for doctors to prescribe.

Colourful Characters

Beam, James Beauregard   He could correctly be described as a true gentleman. In 1896 the *Nelson County Record* wrote of him: 'He is full of energy, stands high as a businessman and no-one is more popular in the community than he.' Praiseworthy qualities for a man whose word was his bond.

Twenty-eight years later, in 1924, he was to prove his honour during a memorable incident. He was in a Bardstown barbershop when the conversation turned to the subject of Prohibition and the havoc it was wreaking on distillery owners. Jim Beam, who was experiencing a difficult time, stated that things were so bad he would sell his Clear Spring distillery to any man who would give him $10,000 immediately. It was ludicrously underpriced but suddenly a voice from the other side of the room confirmed that he would accept. The response had come from Will Styles, a notorious gambler, who just happened to be able to produce the cash at that very moment. Others present knew that Jim Beam had made a disastrous error, but he insisted on keeping his word. Legal records show that an immediate power of attorney was given to Styles who, in the following 12 months, sold the warehouse stock, apparently to Canadian interests, for around $400,000.

Jim Beam is still remembered by his local community as the most honourable of men and his name, more than any other, is seen on bottles of Kentucky Bourbon. (See **Booker Noe**.)

Brooks, Alfred   The B in J & B never met the J, who was an Italian called Giacomo Justerini (see below) who had left England 71 years before Brooks purchased the London wine and spirit business of Johnson & Justerini from Augustus Johnson in 1831. Brooks simply replaced the name Johnson with his own.

He was perhaps something of a dandy, a cross between a country gentleman and a bon viveur, as well as an enthusiastic collector of art and porcelain. He lived a life of luxury in a commodious mansion near Mr Thomas Lord's cricket ground, on an estate that was extensive enough to satisfy his penchant for shooting game. Every morning his carriage would take him to Hyde Park to ride on Rotten Row before he attended his office at the corner of Haymarket and Pall Mall. Brooks oversaw the development of one of the most prestigious trade names in the world.

Daniel, Jasper Jack   The legendary Tennessee distiller learnt the basic skills of distillation at seven years of age, working for a whiskey-making Lutheran pastor called Dan Call – Jack's parents had allowed him to be raised by Call in exchange for his board, lodging and pocket money. He learnt all about Tennessee whiskey and the famous 'leeching process' which today is unique to the Jack Daniel distillery. This requires every drop of their whiskey to pass through a bed of maple charcoal to remove the impurities. In 1860 Dan Call came under pressure from the Union Lutheran Church to change his life-style. Probably quite illegally, he sold his still and small business to the 13-year-old

Jack on extended terms; he allowed him to sell the whiskey through a grocery shop and continued to operate it.

Jack Daniel

In 1866, following the Civil War, all distilleries had to be registered and Jack was the first in the country to seize the chance. It was at this point that he moved his distillery to the celebrated site known as 'the Hollow'; he chose it because of the cool spring in a pure limestone cave, which still provides all the needs of the Jack Daniel's distillery.

In 1905 an incident occurred that eventually brought about Jack's death. His nephew, Lem Motlow, was managing day-to-day matters for him when Jack arrived one morning to collect a document from the office safe. Frustrated by a lock that refused to be opened, he kicked the door and injured his large toe. He gradually developed a limp and, four years later, the injury had festered so badly that it resulted in amputation. Sadly it was too late. Two further amputations failed to halt the problem and in October 1911 Lynchburg's most celebrated son breathed his last.

Dewar, Tom   A great Scotch whisky figure, Dewar was one of a number who made their fortunes largely through the happy coincidence of the arrival of blended whisky and the development of steamship travel. Acting on behalf of his small family business in Perth, he ventured south from Scotland to London in 1885 when he was 21. He recalled arriving with 'two introductions. I found one was dead and the other bankrupt.' In the hair-raising 21 years that followed, 'Whisky Tom', as he became known, began as a persuasive salesman, later borrowed £300,000 from the banks, became a pioneer in electrically illuminated advertising hoardings, built a distillery at Aberfeldy and supplied his whisky to the president of the United States.

While he was a guarded admirer of the fairer sex, he and his close friend 'Sir Tea', as his fellow-Scot Sir Thomas Lipton was known, were both bachelors. It was reported that on one occasion Dewar cabled Lipton from a sales trip to an African country: 'Can buy 3 wives here for 6 pounds of Lipton's tea.' The response was: 'Send samples!' Dewar acquired a large estate in Sussex where he bred horses and greyhounds. He claimed to be the first sponsor of national sport in the United Kingdom and provided trophies and awards for a wide variety of competitions. He was also a somewhat inactive member of parliament.

Perhaps his most amusing honour was to be made Baron Dewar in 1919 when the prohibitionist Lloyd George was Britain's prime minister.

Getz, Oscar   The Chicago-born head of Barton Distillers at Bardstown, Kentucky, began his business life in the windy city with a small shop specialising in radio parts. After the Second World War his company bought the old Tom Moore distillery at Bardstown because of its extensive stocks of mature Bourbon and changed the name to Barton. He became a lifelong collector of what he termed 'whiskeyana' – stills, bottles, posters and bric-a-brac – and created one of the world's finest collections. He eventually donated it to the Oscar Getz Museum of Whiskey History at Bardstown. His generosity and enthusiasm have preserved for succeeding generations a fascinating part of their heritage which would otherwise have disappeared.

Jameson, John   To call him the father figure of Irish whiskey is no exaggeration, for he fathered 16 children and was a most paternal employer. Jameson was born in Alloa in Scotland in 1740 and married Margaret Haig of the Scotch whisky dynasty when she was just 16.

They moved to Ireland and in 1780 he founded the Bow Street distillery in Dublin. His paternalism is reflected in the terms of employment he offered. He paid $1\frac{1}{2}$ times the normal rate, provided applicants could meet three conditions. First, they must be married with at least two children; second they must be non-smokers; and third, they must be of temperate behaviour. In addition to generous wages, he provided housing and a hospital clinic for his employees, and looked after their educational welfare of their children.

No doubt his fatherly guidance inspired the John Jameson label to emerge as the one, great ongoing victory in the turbulent story of Irish whiskey. Figures for 1996 show that Jameson has reached the magic one-million-cases mark with a remarkable sales increase of 17.6 per cent world-wide.

Jefferson, Thomas   The American president and man of culture deserves great praise for his connections with wine, but a slap across the wrist for his attitude to whiskey. It was recorded in 1791 that he had a still on his estate at Monticello which made whiskey from 'grain crops of the farm'. The same record reveals his evident dislike of the drink, as he only permitted its consumption by 'workers and overseers on a ration basis primarily during the harvests'. As it appears to have been a raw young spirit, one wonders if its allocation was a privilege or a sedative.

Justerini, Giacomo   In 1749 this young Italian romantic, who worked as an assistant at his uncle's distillery in Bologna, sacrificed a most promising career for the sake of love. He was swept off his feet by an exhilarating young minor opera-singer called Margherita Bellino, a vivacious lady whose ambitions were only surpassed by her enthusiasm. It appears that she told Giacomo that she was travelling to London to appear in 'the Italian Opera House', and that she wanted him to go with her.

Soon after their arrival in Britain it became clear that stardom did not beckon. In fact, Margherita did not even have a part in the chorus. Nevertheless, she did have Giacomo to support her energetic life-style and he, finding his financial reserves dwindling rapidly, decided to set up in business.

The result was a partnership with a young country gentleman named George Johnson; and in 1749 Justerini & Johnson, later Justerini & Brooks, began trading in the Haymarket near the junction with Pall Mall.

Their business soon prospered as the gentry were attracted by their range of unusual essences, liqueurs and other drinks. It seems that one, the future George III, took more than a passing interest, for upon his accession in 1760 he gave the expanding house his royal warrant, a practice which has continued to this day. Curiously, the involvement of Giacomo Justerini lasted a mere 11 years. In 1760 he took a substantial share of the profits and returned to Bologna, but whether to his uncle's distillery or another affair of the heart is unknown.

Johnston, Donald and Alexander   In 1820 Donald and Alexander Johnston opened a distillery on the beach at Laphroaig on the south-west coast of the island of Islay, home to the most distinctive whiskies. The partnership progressed happily for 16 years until a bitter dispute broke out between the brothers. Alexander, the younger, declared he would take his share of their possessions and move a mile away to set up a rival distillery and put Laphroaig out of business by producing an identical whisky. Equipment and staff were divided between the erstwhile partners and Alexander chose his site at Lagavulin, called it Malt Mill and set to work. But no matter how he tried he could not copy the Laphroaig style. He had overlooked the effect of the sea and built his new distillery slightly inland. As a result the Malt Mill whisky never had the same iodine bouquet for which Laphroaig was so famous.

Tragically, Donald lost his life in 1847 when he fell into his burnt-ale vat. Fortunately, the brothers' differences had long been resolved.

Lloyd Price, Richard John Best known as R.J. Lloyd Price, he was both an extrovert and an entrepreneur who dabbled in many imaginative schemes. The local squire, he lived in an old stone mansion called Rhiwlas-Bala, near Bala in North Wales, and claimed to have founded the world's first sheepdog trials. He was also a successful racehorse-owner and, in the 1870s and 1880s, operated a remunerative business delivering fresh game and poultry to London by the night train. Among his recreations was membership of various gentlemen's clubs in London where he enjoyed a wee dram.

He knew that there was a history of sporadic efforts to produce Welsh whiskey and decided to revive the tradition. So on 3 June 1889, apparently with some support from the Haig whisky family who were then extremely successful in Scotland, the sum of £100,000 was raised to form the Welsh Whiskey Distillery Co. Ltd. As part of the arrangement Lloyd Price sold the company a parcel of his land at Frongoch, and water in the Tairvelin brook and Tryweryn river.

A substantial distillery was built in addition to stone warehouses and cottages for employees. Sadly, less than 11 years later the business was sold 'in liquidation' to William Owen of the White Lion Hotel, Bala, for £5000. His efforts, too, were of no avail and in 1907 production ceased. By 1914 the distillery had been converted into the Frongoch prisoner-of-war camp for Germans and later became a concentration camp to hold internees during the Irish uprising.

The reason for the distillery's failure was simple. It produced a full-flavoured single malt at a time when the lighter style of blended Scotch whisky had transformed the international markets and made it the world's favourite drink.

Noe, Booker   The maternal grandson of the more famous Jim Beam, he is in effect the man who helped his grandfather become a celebrated international name. At around 6 feet 4 inches (1–93m) and 21 stone 6 lbs (300 pounds/136 kilograms), Booker is a big man, stout in heart and body. He tells – with moist eyes – how in 1948, when he was 17, his fading 84-year-old grandfather called him to his room and gave him his favourite pump-action shotgun. Thus manhood arrived and, in due course, Booker helped to make Jim Beam into one of the most successful brands on earth. He developed a light, clean style of Kentucky Bourbon that offered new possibilities as it mixed well in long drinks. More recently, a mature special selection Bourbon called Booker's has been launched. Strangely, Booker has travelled most of the whisky-producing countries of the world but for some unexplained reason has never been to Scotland.

Samuels, Bill The president of Maker's Mark, he is one of the only two individuals still alive (the other is Booker Noe) who cannot be denied entry in this chapter. He is one of the great story-tellers of his generation and nowadays gives the impression that he believes every word of his many tales. He is also a keen practical joker who, on one occasion at the annual Kentucky Derby at Churchill Downs, hired a diminutive Jack Daniel look-alike and instructed him to offer guests free glasses of Maker's Mark. A remarkably youthful figure for his age – approaching 60 – Bill is a fine advertisement for a superb Kentucky Bourbon.

There is just a tiny bit of confusion concerning his much-publicised Scots–Irish heritage, for a photograph exists of a claimed ancestor called Reuben Samuels who appears to be dressed as an orthodox Jewish rabbi. It may just be a jest the opposition played on him!

Seagram, Joseph Emms Much has been written about the Seagram company, and the Bronfman family who have controlled it since Prohibition days, but considerably less is known about its true founder, Joseph E. Seagram. When Joseph's father Octavius was 19, in 1887, he eloped to Canada from Bratton in Wiltshire with Amelia Stiles, the daughter of John Stiles, an estate worker. John and his family suffered the wrath of William Ballard Seagram, father of Octavius and the squire of Bratton House, who evicted them from their cottage and demolished it.

Joseph was born at Hespeler, Upper Canada (Ontario), in 1841 and was orphaned when he was 11. Following the death of his father in 1848 his mother had married a storekeeper, John Barbour, and Joseph and his brother Edward were extremely fortunate that their stepfather treated them as his own and had them educated at a grammar school in the neighbouring town of Galt. At 15 Joseph bought his first racehorse and entered it in races under another person's name. After leaving school he studied business at a college in Buffalo, New York.

In 1864 he started work at the Waterloo distillery, Canada, which had been founded in 1857, and by 1883 he was the outright owner with 40 employees making 4.5 million litres (1,188,806 US gallons) of whisky in that year alone. He became a multimillionaire and owned nearly a hundred racehorses, yet never possessed a car.

His interest in racing matched his enthusiasm for his whisky business. His black-and-yellow racing colours could be seen at tracks all over Canada and the eastern United States. Every time he had a winner he wired the result to the distillery and the Union Jack was raised to the top of its flagpole.

When middle-aged he wore a full beard and moustache, and his portly but smartly dressed figure was extremely well known. In July 1903 The *New York Morning Telegraph* asked: 'Do you know Joseph Seagram? If you do not, go out to the race track and pick out the man who looks like King Edward VII . . . that man is Seagram.'

In 1907, he asked his head distiller, William Hortrop, to provide a special blend of older whiskies for his son Thomas's wedding. He was so delighted with the result that it became a new brand under the name Very Own which became abbreviated to V.O.

In 1926 his sons and successors floated the company on the stock market. The Montreal-based Bronfman brothers obtained control following stock acquisitions in 1928 and 1929.

Teacher, Adam Business trips in the nineteenth century were not quite what they are today, although a voyage in 1871 by a 32-year-old partner in the famous Scotch whisky company Wm. Teacher & Sons was perhaps slightly more unorthodox than most. Teacher sailed from Glasgow with a zoologist friend, Ian Campbell, on board a guano-carrying barque, the *Tumuri*, destined for South America.

After reaching St Vincent they headed south to Rio de Janeiro and then Montevideo in Uruguay. There the promising export director indulged himself in regular theatre-going, skating and billiards – and incurred a costly hotel bill of nearly £21 in just 24 days. He did manage the odd appointment, but strangely all of them seem to have been with people with Scottish names.

A week after sailing from Montevideo his log described his activities with Campbell. They caught gulls which they skinned, soaked with arsenic and peppered to deter rats. Then, ignoring his childhood poetry, Adam attempted – and failed – to shoot an albatross or two, but killed a friendly Cape pigeon instead.

The twenty-fourth of November 1871 was a day to remember. The two friends slaughtered two sheep and, to save fodder, ate sheep's head broth and haggis and recorded that their shipboard zoo consisted of 14 sheep, two pigs, two dogs, three cats, a canary and innumerable rats. Campbell, who did not appear to have done much serious work, was said to be, 'anxious to get [an] Indian for specimen' and 'thinks arsenical soup would preserve his principal parts'.

To make matters worse the captain was a persistent drunkard, the ship was hit by, and survived, a hurricane and there was a near mutiny. The *Tumuri* was finally shipwrecked with the loss of 400 sacks of guano, and the 'expedition' sailed home on her sister ship.

It is believed that Adam subsequently became domiciled in Glasgow and was always reluctant to leave.

Walker, Hiram   Born and raised in Massachusetts, Hiram Walker always had an inclination for the whiskey trade. The imposition of Prohibition in Massachusetts in 1838 (see **Prohibition**) saw him travel west to the small town of Detroit where, aged 22, he opened a business as a licensed grocer. He later started trading in cereals and this took him across the Detroit river to Upper Canada (Ontario) where in 1856, at the age of 40, he built the Windsor

Distillery and Flour Mill. Initially, his whiskey production was spasmodic but it soon grew sufficiently for him to concentrate on the venture.

He continued to live in Detroit and crossed the river each day to run business on both sides of the border. By the mid-1860s his great plan was under way. On the river bank in Windsor he developed Walkerville, an entire community centred around his distillery, which supplied jobs, homes and recreation for his employees and their families. A Walkerville post office was sanctioned and Hiram Walker even provided a school and church.

He later achieved great success with his Canadian Club brand and was awarded the royal warrant by Queen Victoria in 1898, just one year before his death at the age of 83. He left behind a philanthropic legacy that can still be visited today.

Walker, Johnnie   A grocer in Kilmarnock, Scotland, Johnnie Walker's name graces the blended premium Scotch whisky that is the No. 1 world-seller. In 1820 he founded a shop for provisions plus wines and spirits. In those days the only whisky he sold would have been single malt from the cask. In fact, it was his ambitious son, Alexander, who made him famous: when blended whiskies became the fashion he created a blend which carried his father's name. In 1880 Alexander began trading in London and was soon exporting his whisky all over the world. Trade legend suggests that it achieved its fame by the advertising line 'Born 1820 still going strong' – which has little bearing on the blend.

Washington, George   The first president of the United States built his own distillery in 1787 alongside his farm at Dogue, near his Mount Vernon estate. It had five pot stills, one constructed by Robert Bush and Co., still-manufacturers of 20 High Street, Bristol, England. The distillery was managed by a Scotsman called James Anderson. Rye, wheat, Indian corn and other grains were used though there is no specific mention of barley. In 1789 Washington reported a profit of $1032. One of his stills survives in the Bureau of Alcohol, Tobacco and Firearms Bicentennial Museum in Washington, DC.

Williams, Evan   In 1783 Williams built Kentucky's first commercial whisky distillery in Louisville, on the right bank of the Ohio river, near the junction of Fifth and Water Street, in an area then known as Ohio Falls. His grandparents had owned the only recorded eighteenth-century whiskey distillery in Wales and had emigrated to Prince William County, Virginia, in 1707.

In 1892, more than a hundred years after the distillery had been built, Colonel Reuben T. Durrett, Kentucky's first historian, wrote that Evan Williams 'distilled whisky from corn', and that it was 'a good medicine for chills and fever, though a very bad whisky'. Williams was also a builder, and for a period harbour master – in which role he clashed with William Johnston, the port surveyor. For some years both men were members of the Louisville Board of Trustees, supervising the municipal requirements of a 500-strong population, and it was in this capacity that their views on whiskey clashed.

On one occasion Williams thought it 'the handsome thing to bring a bottle of his own make of whisky for the members to enjoy'. Johnston, who was the clerk, confiscated it under rule 7 and it was returned when the meeting had concluded. All the members tasted the whiskey with apparent satisfaction, but when Johnston sipped it he declared it was 'too mean to be drunk', and that, 'Williams ought to be expelled from the Board for making such villainous stuff'.

Nowadays the Evan Williams brand is distilled at the Heaven Hill distillery in Bardstown, where it is matured and blended to make an extremely smooth eight-year-old Bourbon, quite a step from a crude young corn whisky.

Williamson, Bessie (Elizabeth Leitch) In 1932 Bessie Williamson graduated in pharmacy at Glasgow University but, because of the state of the economy and the preference given to employing men, she was unable to obtain a suitable position and was forced to work as a shorthand secretary. The following summer she accepted the invitation of a fellow woman student to share a short holiday on the island of Islay in the Inner Hebrides. As both were total abstainers they stayed in the Temperance Hotel in Port Ellen. Yet Dame Fortune was about to wave her wand, for Bessie Williamson became the first woman to be both a head distiller and distillery owner in Scotland.

Bessie overheard someone in a shop telling her friend that the secretary of Iain Hunter, the owner of the Laphroaig distillery, was ill and that he was anxiously searching for a temporary secretary who could take shorthand. The friend suggested to Bessie that she offer her assistance and the young pharmacist, curious to observe distillation on a major scale, immediately volunteered.

The regular secretary returned three days later, but Bessie never left the distillery. She so impressed Hunter with her enthusiasm that he made her his assistant and taught her the skills of distilling. When he travelled to the mainland or abroad he would place her in charge. Years later he became seriously ill and appointed Bessie head distiller, and when he died he bequeathed Laphroaig to her. She died in 1982, no longer a total abstainer but always temperate.

Although Bessie never married, she had a long-standing relationship with a radio entertainer called Wishart Campbell, known as the 'golden voice of Canadian air'.

The Word Whisky

It can be no coincidence that the term 'water of life' occurs in so many European languages. Throughout the British Isles, before the word 'whisky' was in common usage, the Latin *aqua vitae* meaning 'water of life' was the accepted legal name for spirits. The Spanish have their *aguardiente*, the Portuguese *aguardente*, the French *eau-de-vie*, Scandinavians have *aquavit* and the Poles and Russians their *vodka*. All translate as 'water of life' as do *usquebaugh* and *usque beatha*. *Usque* is of Celtic derivation and is related to the Welsh word *wysg* for running water, still seen today in the name of the River Usk in Gwent.

In Scotland usquebaugh is often said to be Irish or slang, and *uisge beatha* (pronounced 'ooshka beha') is suggested as the correct form. However, the writer Martin Martin in his 1703 *Description of the Western Isles of Scotland* referred to usquebaugh, as did Dr Johnson in his dictionary.

Today *The Oxford Dictionary* lists nine variations of usquebaugh and refers to examples like *uskeaghe*, from Derricke's *Image of Ireland* (1581) and Sir R. Cecil Lett of Camden (London) who, in 1600, wrote of the Lord Treasurer owning 'some *uscough baugh*'. It also quotes a 1682 *London Gazette* report that, 'there is right Irish Usquebaugh to be sold . . . at the Rein Deer in Turtle Street'.

Much has been written about how the soldiers of Henry II of England shortened usquebaugh, which they found difficult to pronounce, to whisky when they invaded Ireland in 1171–72, but actual evidence is elusive.

Legend suggests that Irish monks, who travelled to and from the Mediterranean during the sixth and seventh centuries, returned with the secret of distillation, but there is no written evidence. Various writers have stated that the process began with the Arabs in the eleventh century but, again, this is difficult to prove.

Many have overlooked the fact that in the first century BC Greek sailors used a simple form of distillation when they suspended sponges over pots of boiling sea water to absorb the salt-free steam – when this condensed it could be wrung out of the sponges as fresh water. Records also suggest that the Romans used distillation to extract turpentine.

Greek seamen before Christ had long been familiar with the eastern and central Mediterranean, but they gradually ventured west and drifted into the Atlantic, then braved longer journeys northwards, intent on trading in new markets. So could they not have taken their simple art of distillation and shared it with others? Doubters say, of course, that no remains of any apparatus have been found – but if sponges were used there would be no trace of them.

Alongside this, the development of all spirits distilled from cereals should be considered. In simple terms, a mash can be made from water mixed with corn (maize), rye or barley (malted or not), and its fermentation encouraged to make a basic beer. This is then distilled to produce a clear alcoholic spirit. At this stage the spirit can, if desired, be adapted to produce a variety of drinks, the best known of which are vodka, gin and whisky. To produce vodka, the young spirit is filtered through charcoals; to make gin, juniper, coriander and other botanicals are added; but whisky must be matured in oak casks, many of which may be charred. It is this ageing that gives whisky its style and character, qualities which, at their peak, cannot be surpassed by any other spirit.

Usquebaugh or early whisky was consumed very young and was often extremely unpalatable. Two main methods were used to overcome this. One was triple distillation, known as *trestarig*, or even quadruple distillation. The drawback to crude multiple distillation was that it usually resulted in a very dull liquor lacking in flavour. The other remedy was to compound the spirit with a concoction of herbs and spices to add flavouring. (Interestingly, Swn-y-Mor, the only Welsh whisky, still employs this technique today.) Occasionally, distillers would adjust the flavour by adding other spirits such as rum.

Compounding clearly became commonplace, for in 1729 G. Smith of Kendal, Westmoreland, provided a recipe for making 'fine usquebaugh' in

A Compleat Body of Distilling, the first English manual of its type. It was somewhat complicated with the ingredients being comprised of 'molasses spirits [rum], malt spirits, Mace, Cloves, Nutts, Cinnamon, Coriander, Ginger, Cubebs, English Saffron, Raisins, Dates and Lisbon Sugar'.

The arguments over the derivation of the word 'whisky' and the origins of distillation are destined to continue because of the lack of conclusive written or archaeological evidence. However, they are a fascinating area of research which requires zeal and dedication.

The Mythical

'E'

In this book an *e* is generally used in the spelling of whiskey from Ireland and the United States of America.

The debate about its use is not new. It has often been suggested that the *e* came from the original spelling of the word 'whiskey' in Ireland and was later taken to North America by Scots-Irish settlers. It arrived in Kentucky as those emigrants headed west.

However, practice does not always support theory. An 1896 price list for Victoria Wine, the first multiple wine and drink retailer in Great Britain, spells the word without an *e* on nine occasions when referring to the Irish spirit. An advertising poster of the same era from the Dublin Whisky Distillery Co. uses the word twice without an *e*, as does a similar later poster for the Phoenix Park distillery. Across the Atlantic the *Nelson County Record of Bardstown, Kentucky*, in a special 1896 edition, contains a comprehensive history and background to nearly 40 local distillers and always spells the word with an *e*, with the exception of two items in one sketch of three barrels. Furthermore, historians agree that the Scots–Irish were largely responsible for the birth of Canadian whisky. Yet in Canada the word has virtually always been spelt without an *e*.

In contrast Dickens, in his *Sketches by Boz*, used an *e*, as in 'he went home . . . for his whiskey and water'. In 1795 Thomas Carneal, acting for the United States Federal Government, issued a notice that he needed 'a quantity of Whisk*eu*, for the use of the army, for which cash will be offered in payment'. In 1814 a Louisville, Kentucky, store announced its sale of 'Rye Whiskey'. An 1877 advertisement for Geo. Roe & Co.'s Dublin Whiskey spells the word with an *e* on eight occasions.

In 1889 the Kentucky historian Colonel Reuben T. Durret, writing about Evan Williams and his 1783 distillery, used *whisky*, something he surely would not have done if the *e* was then in common use. Two years earlier Alfred Barnard, in his *Whisky Distilleries of the United Kingdom*, wrote of 28 distilleries he had visited in Ireland and never once used an *e*. In their 1896 list John Harvey & Sons Ltd of Bristol, England, offered seven items under Irish *Whisky*.

The situation remains confused, as neither the Paddy label from Ireland, George Dickel from

Tennessee or Maker's Mark, Old Forester and Early Times from Kentucky use an e.

The plural of whisky is whiskies, but the plural of whiskey is whiskeys. This makes it very difficult to provide a generic plural in countries or states where both spellings are used.

Spelling whisky with or without an e appears to be largely a matter of human whim.

Chronology

1st century BC   Greek sailors used a basic form of distillation when they obtained pure fresh water by draping sponges over pots of boiling sea water.

circa 350–400 AD   According to legend, Realt Hir, a Celtic chieftain, distilled a fiery spirit from barley beer on Bardsey Island, North Wales.

7th century AD   Geber the Arab wrote the first known description of the apparatus used in distillation, but only referred to obtaining fragrant extracts from plants and flowers.

11th century AD   This is the much-quoted, but somewhat vague, date given for first reports of Arabs using distillation to produce the cosmetic kohl.

1175   Henry II's English soldiers are said to have anglicised *uisce* into whisky after they had invaded Ireland.

1276   Sir Thomas Savage, of Bushmills in Northern Ireland, 'fortified his troops going into battle with a mighty draft of *uisce beatha*'.

1494   The Scottish Exchequer Rolls refers to a permit for the Benedictine friar John Cor to purchase four bolls (six bushels) of barley to distil *aqua vitae* for James IV of Scotland.

1577   In his *Chronicles of England, Scotland and Ireland*, Raphael Holinshed wrote of the beneficial properties of *uisge beatha*.

1617   Sir Walter Raleigh recorded a gift of a 32

gallon (145 litre) keg of uisce beatha from the earl of Cork.

1640 Wilhelm Hendriksen produced a corn and rye whisky on Staten Island, then part of the Dutch colony of New Netherland.

1644 The Scottish parliament imposed the world's first excise tax on whisky: of 2 shillings and 8 pence per Scottish pint.

1725 *A Compleat Body of Distilling explaining the Mysteries of that Science* by G. Smith of Kendal, Westmoreland, was published. It is the first known textbook on the subject in the British Isles.

1761 Bristol Malt Whisky was served in public celebrations for the visit of the duke of York.

1779 Justerini & Johnson, later Justerini & Brooks, placed the first known whisky advertisement. In the *Morning Post and Daily Advertiser*, in London, they announced the arrival of various drinks including Usquebaugh.

1779 The Distilling Act caused problems in Ireland where there were over 1152 known stills. In 1790 there were 250.

1787   The first record of George Washington as a distiller. (See **Colourful Characters**.)

1794   The first Canadian tax on stills was imposed by John Graves Simcoe, the lieutenant governor of Upper Canada (Ontario), on behalf of the British government.

1799   The Molsom family, famed for beer, opened the first commercial whisky distillery in Canada, in Montreal. (See **Canada**.)

1830   Aeneas Coffey, a former customs and Excise inspector, patented his continuous still in Ireland.

1849   Earliest known sale of bottled Bourbon by Bininger's, a New York City grocery store.

1875   Gilbey's, the largest wine and spirit merchant in the British Isles, sold 996,000 bottles of Irish whiskey compared with 456,000 bottles of Scotch.

1898   161 licensed distilleries were operating in Scotland.

1920–33   Prohibition was in force in the United States.

1923   The first Japanese whisky distillery was established, near Kyoto in the vale of Yamazaki.

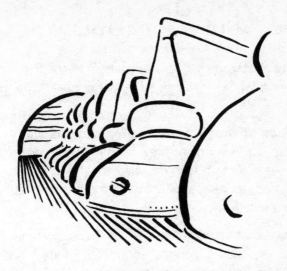

1987 The Cooley distillery was the first to open in Ireland in the twentieth century.

1996 New Zealand permitted domestic pot stills.

Did You Know?

The Antiquary This outstanding Scotch deluxe whisky was named after the novel written by Sir Walter Scott in 1816.

birds of prey Some distilleries in Scotland have stuffed birds of prey, fixed in flying positions above the mash tuns or wherever else they are needed, to deter small birds that otherwise might be a health hazard.

bowls at work The Glenkinchie distillery in the Lowlands region just south of Edinburgh has its own bowling green which can be used by visitors as well as the distillery's own team. It is a remnant of an old tradition started by the now-forgotten Yoker Scotch whisky distillery, which was founded in 1770 amidst attractive surroundings on the banks of the Clyde. The Harvey family who built it were considerate employers and provided their employees with a superb bowling green.

the company store Apparently the scourge of American miners who had to spend wage tokens in the company's own shop, it was also a harsh reality in parts of Scotland for distillery workers who never saw actual cash. They were obliged to exchange their tokens for oats, barley, candles and general provisions supplied by the owners. Examples of the tokens can still be seen at the Talisker distillery on Skye, though nowadays the employees there are completely free from such abuse.

choosing a site In Scotland many old

distilleries were built on the sites of former illegal operations. Glendronach, positioned amidst a rather lively rookery, was a prime example. Apparently its previous unlicensed occupants chose the setting because the birds made a dreadful racket if anyone came close to it.

The site for the Aberlour distillery on Speyside may well have been selected on religious grounds. In 1879 its founder, James Fleming, a man of saintly and most generous reputation, chose it for four reasons: it was in a sheltered valley known as a glen and it was near a spring, an abundant supply of oak and a navigable river. For identical reasons, St Drostan, the nephew of St Colomba, had chosen the very same spot for a Christian settlement early in the seventh century. Today the Aberlour distillery uses Saint Drostan's Well where, it is believed, he baptised the first Highland chiefs to become Christians. On St Drostan's Day, 11 July, every lover of Aberlour is called upon to partake of whisky and water at 8.00 a.m., 4.00 p.m. and midnight.

A neighbouring coal mine was the reason for selecting the site of the Clynelish distillery (originally called Brora), founded by the marquis of Stafford in 1819 in north-east Scotland. But it was a dreadful blunder: the coal was of the wrong type and produced insufficient heat to fire the stills.

Japanese whisky inspiration In 1919, when Japan did not possess a single distillery, an enquiring young Japanese student called Masataka Takasuru obtained employment in Rothes, in the heart of the Speyside region of Scotland, where he married a local girl. He

showed great interest in the construction of
distillery equipment, and the local coppersmith,
Forsyth & Sons, allowed him to make drawings of
various items. He returned to Japan and joined
Suntory, the first Japanese whisky company. In
1934 he founded his own company called Yoichi
Hokkaido, later renamed the Nikka Whisky
Distilling Company. Today it owns the Ben Nevis
distillery among other interests.

**Marconi had Jameson in his
blood**   Guglielmo Marconi, the celebrated
radio pioneer, was the great-grandson of John
Jameson, the Irish whiskey founder. In about
1860 Annie Jameson, John's granddaughter,
dreamed of being an opera star and travelled to
Bologna, in what was about to become Italy. There
she married Giuseppe Marconi in 1864. Her
inventor son carried out many of his successful
experiments in Ireland.

Paddy was a salesman   Paddy whisky from
Ireland, which does not use an *e*, was named
after Paddy O'Flaherty, an extremely popular sales
representative of Cork distilleries in the early
1920s. He produced outstanding sales for Fine Old
Cork Whiskey after it had failed to make much
progress. He was so successful that his customers
nicknamed it 'Paddy's whisky'. The company
subsequently renamed it after him.

a singleton   This is an old Scottish term for
one remaining cask of single malt – hence the
identity of the Speyside distillery The Singleton of
Auchroisk. It was considered that the village
name of Auchroisk, pronounced 'Orthrusk', would

cause problems for consumers and The Singleton was added.

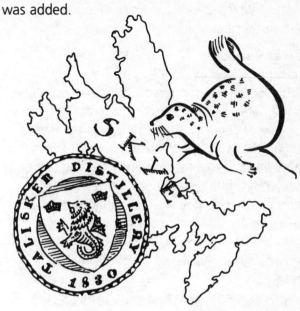

the Talisker seal   On the island of Skye, off the north-west coast of Scotland, in the tiny village of Carbost, one finds the Talisker distillery where a delightfully peppery, peaty malt is produced. On most summer days at noon 'the Talisker seal' makes his visit to the Loch Harport coastline and swims alongside a buoy that marks exactly where the warm, surplus, distillery water enters the sea. Some of the distillery workers are part-time lobster-pot men and report that the fattest lobsters are caught at the same spot.

floating out the barrels   Another Talisker tale tells how MacLeod, the local landlord refused to allow a pier to be constructed on Loch Harport. Until the mid-twentieth century distillery workers literally had to float the barrels, towing them from a small boat, some 400 yards (365 metres) to 'puffers' which shipped them to Glasgow and even farther away.

water sources   Every whisky in the world attaches great importance to its water supply. In Kentucky Jim Beam refers to its 'sweet limestone water', while on the island of Islay, the Bowmore distillery emphasises the peatiness of the River Laggan that supplies its needs. While water is by no means the sole factor influencing the character of a whisky, it is a crucial one. For example, a valley could have three neighbouring distilleries yet the water for the first might run over sandstone, the second over granite and the third over limestone. All would produce different results.

When Justerini & Brooks were planning the construction of their Auchroisk distillery in the early 1970s, they transported water from Dorie's Well to their nearby Glen Spey distillery and carried out trial distillations. The analysis of the new spirit convinced them that attractive characteristics would be found in their new Singleton of Auchroisk single malt.

The Excise Man

the excise man   A much vilified character, he
was often regarded as a traitor by his neighbours.
Gradually, as the taxation laws were accepted, the
necessity of his role was begrudgingly
acknowledged.

Because the quality of water sources was
already established, many new distilleries were
built where old illicit operations had once
flourished, and eventually most production came
under the excise man's control.

When Trader Control was introduced in 1988,
Her Majesty's Customs and Excise officers
withdrew from distilleries in Scotland, ending a
symbiotic relationship between them and
distillery staff in which certain unofficial standards
of give-and-take were accepted.

checking the hydrometers   At a Speyside
distillery in the second half of this century, an
excise officer always carried out a monthly check
on the efficacy of the Sykes hydrometer by
comparing it with a spare instrument that was
kept in perfect condition. This recognised
procedure necessitated filling a flask large enough
to hold both hydrometers with whisky. Curiously,
the whisky sample was never taken from the new
spirit but always from a 12- or 15-year-old malt.
The flask was taken back to the Customs and
Excise on-site office and its contents somehow
never returned to their source. Some believed that
the whisky always left the premises that same
day in the officer's small brown leather case – for
official purposes, of course!

flowing over the border In the early 1820s the brewers and wine and spirit merchants of Carlisle, about 15 miles (24 kilometres) south of the Scottish border, reported that 'between 8–11,000 gallons a week were crossing the border'. Their published complaint described the illicit Scotch whisky as 'liquor of the vilest description, retailing at 6 shillings a gallon'.

Every imaginable method of concealment was used. One popular trick was to train a dog to follow a regular route, carrying two pigs' bladders full of illicit whisky. Dogs were rewarded for swimming across the Esk and Eden rivers – if the smugglers saw an excise man approaching they threw their dogs into the water, thereby saving their whisky.

So-called 'women of spirit' wore voluminous clothes to hide containers. Carlisle Museum has a 'belly canteen' which was strapped to a young woman to give the impression that she was pregnant, and filled with 9 litres (2 gallons) of whisky.

the man with the limp A distillery manager in Aberdeenshire, Scotland, felt sympathetic towards a new excise man who had a pronounced limp and always struggled from his car to his office, and between the various warehouses.

For 20 years the excise man remained aloof. He travelled from a town a considerable distance away and never conversed or mingled socially with distillery staff. One weekend the manager happened to visit the excise man's home town and by chance saw him walking, without any sign of a limp, along the High Street. Apparently a metal pipe concealed within the official's trouser leg caused the limp – and it was always heavier when he left the distillery than when he arrived.

the old stag's horn This was used as an agreed measure at the Talisker distillery on Skye. Twice a day the brewer, with the active approval of the customs officer, filled a copper 'dramming cask' from a suitable barrel and shared out the samples using the hollow horn as a measure.

hokonui New Zealand's most popular moonshine from the 1860s to the 1930s was named after the Hokonui range of mountains. The most famous illicit distiller was one James Quirk, a local hero known as 'Bottling Quirk' who was put on trial for illicit distillation in 1934. He was found not guilty and returned to a banner-waving street reception in his home town of Mataura. Another unidentified distiller who named himself 'Me' listed police officers and judges among his clientele. His Old Hokonui labels carried a skull and crossbones, a guarantee that the spirit was 'free from poisons' and 'supplied to snake charmers' and displayed the Latin motto *Ergo Bibamus* (so let's drink).

Moonshining came to New Zealand with settlers from Scotland and it is reputed that during the first half of the twentieth century Hokonui became as widespread there as *poitìn* was in Ireland. One notorious opponent was H.S. Cordery, the collector of Customs. He was known as the 'Hammer of the Scots', a title justified by his sledgehammer destruction of the numerous stills he discovered.

In 1996 an enlightened New Zealand government introduced new legislation permitting any citizen to operate a private still, free of licence and excise tax. This has led to the world's first radio commercials offering pot stills for home use, complete with instructions. Despite this, a Yugoslav-owned moonshine operation only 20 minutes drive from Auckland still thrives. Customers appear to be drawing hot water from a wash-house boiler, but when they press the cold tap they receive a constant flow of whisky.

poitìn (poteen)   Poitìn in Ireland, and the smuggled malts in other parts of the British Isles, were much fuller in flavour than the rectified spirits that were widely available. Rectification – refining spirits through repeated distillation – meant that vast volumes of bland spirits flooded the market and as a result consumers sought to find something with more flavour. For that very reason, many refer to poitìn as 'the good stuff' in areas where you can still buy it. It is still produced in illicit stills in the Republic of Ireland and Northern Ireland. Quite sophisticated commercial organisations often distribute it through other reputable businesses.

Robert Burns   Scotland's national poet had a rather ambivalent attitude towards the excise man and may appear to some to have been a turncoat. In *The De'il's awa' wi' the Exciseman* he had harsh words to say about the job which he himself was employed to do. The circumstances in which the song was composed help to shed some light on his feelings: he was hiding a marsh, in the most miserable conditions, observing a suspect boat.

Aeneas Coffey   In 1824 Coffey resigned as inspector general of excise in Ireland and took over the Dock Street distillery in Dublin. In 1830, aged 50, he patented his continuous column still. This produced a constant supply of inexpensive grain spirit, which distillers blended with malts to set the new trend for lighter, blended whiskies. Ironically, this was to bring about the sudden growth of blended Scotch whisky and subsequently the demise of many distilleries in Ireland.

Prohibition

Prohibition was first attempted by King Burebista of Thrace in 50 BC in his capital city of Deva, now in modern Romania. He was stabbed to death in his palace by his priests in 44 BC, the same year in which Julius Caesar was assassinated.

Prior to the arrival of the Spanish, the Aztecs tried to impose Prohibition and it was adopted to some degree in China, Polynesia, Japan, India, Russia, Finland and Sweden before it was ever considered in North America. In all instances it was a signal failure.

The first limited United States temperance law was invoked in Massachusetts in 1838 but was repealed two years later. In 1846 Maine became the first state to impose Prohibition on a long-term basis. Thirty years later the Prohibition party began its campaign for national prohibition and Kansas declared itself 'dry' in 1880. By 1890 six more states had banned the demon drink. In 1903 the bar of the Capitol building in Washington, DC, was closed down and by 1910 the movement was in full spate even in the main whiskey-producing states.

On 16 January 1920 Prohibition came into effect in the United States, made law by the Volstead Act which was eventually repealed on 5 December 1933. The law provoked widespread defiance and numerous examples of human ingenuity and eccentric conduct.

Prosecutions were rarely successful as juries were normally reluctant to convict their fellow men of offences that they too were committing regularly. Consequently, in 1921 only 18 of 1422 cases brought resulted in convictions. In 1922, 2318 of 2733 cases were dismissed and in 1923, 2462 out of 2739.

And it was all to little or no avail. In 1930 the number of illicit stills confiscated rose to a staggering 282,122. Basic stills were not expensive to make and represented a rapid and generous profit. The moment one was seized, a replacement would be constructed.

Prohibition brought certain colourful individuals to the fore. The examples given here are generally associated with whiskey.

Izzy and Moe The opposition to Prohibition was so widespread that 95,933 illegal operations were uncovered in 1921, varying from tiny stills in backyard sheds to full-scale grain distilleries hidden on the premises of businesses otherwise presumed to be respectable. Prohibition agents were employed to uncover illicit stills, locate speakeasies and catch smugglers. Two of the most successful were Isadore Einstein and Moe Smith, best known as Izzy and Moe. They were both corpulent characters, Izzy being particularly recognisable at just 5 feet 6 inches high (1.7 metres) and 16 st (225 pounds/102 kilograms).

In five years they made 4392 arrests and seized some five million bootleg bottles. New York journalist Paul Sann wrote that their job was literally 'to pour whiskey down drains'. On one occasion Izzy chanced to meet Albert Einstein and told him, 'I'm a discover too, only I discover in basements.'

the Canadian border   The USA/Canada border is 6400 kilometres (3986 miles) long and as a result gave the Canadians a memorable opportunity to prosper at the expense of their American neighbours. Despite its length, records indicate that around 80 per cent of liquor-smuggling occurred over a few miles of the St Clair river (also known as the Detroit river), through what was known as the Windsor–Detroit funnel.

The United States land and sea borders total nearly 19,000 miles (30,600 kilometres) and at the peak of Prohibition the Coast Guard and Customs Service employed less than 3000 agents. Assuming that every agent worked eight hours a day, this meant that each shift would have had to cover nearly 19 miles (30 kilometres) of frontier. Uncle Sam never stood a chance.

Much has been written about smuggling whisky from Canada to the United States across the Great Lakes and on the eastern seaboard, but far less has been recorded about activities on the west coast. Distilleries in British Columbia and Saskatchewan provided a steady stream of Canadian and Scotch whisky for the consumers of Washington, Oregon, Idaho, California and surrounding states, often on ships which formed rows along the entire coast from Seattle to San Diego. Since the west coast had, in those days, a much smaller population than the states in the east, the overall trade was much less. Many large American cars proved particularly strong workhorses, carrying several dozen cases on a quick dash across the border at some remote point – where, in any case, the customs officers may have been on the runners' payroll.

Initially, United States coast guards were ill-equipped and could do little to interrupt the trade, but by the mid-1920s Uncle Sam's organisation was greatly improved and it became necessary for smuggling to be somewhat more sophisticated.

Few non-Canadians realise that various states of Canada had their own forms of Prohibition, some of which were strange to say the least. Ontario was more involved in whisky running than any other states even during its own dry era which lasted from 1917 until the very last city, Owen Sound, went wet in 1972. It was perfectly legal to export whisky to other countries provided they were not also under Prohibition. So stocks would be documented for Mexico or Venezuela, then transported by rail to Detroit. Here they would be passed for their forward journey, only to be lost somewhere before the Mexican border. Somewhere, of course, usually meant within 8 kilometres (5 miles) of entering the USA.

In response to calls from the United States authorities for better co-operation from Canada, the *Ottawa Journal* wrote, on one occasion, that 'US enforcement, like charity, should begin at home'.

the Bronfmans, Seagrams and Prohibition   Despite the efforts of the US Coast Guard Service on the Great Lakes, most of the contraband arrived intact. An amusing tale is told of the Bronfman operation, in the early days of Prohibition before they had acquired the Seagram company. If the smugglers were spotted by a coastguard while they were at sea they would throw the whisky overboard in sacks attached to blocks of salt and take a careful compass bearing. They would return 8–10 hours later to find that the salt had dissolved and the bottle floated to the surface; they merely had to re-label them.

Curiously, the legendary Samuel Bronfman, widely known as 'Mr Sam', was for many years reluctant to acknowledge that a substantial part of the family fortune had come from Prohibition. In *From Little Acorns*, a Seagram book that he wrote and published in 1970, he avoided the matter and apparently preferred not to discuss the topic with enquirers. Yet in his last years he began to make various references to the subject. In *Mr Sam, The Life and Time of Samuel Bronfman* by Michael R. Marros, he is said to have admitted: 'We were late starters in the two most lucrative markets – on the high seas and across the Detroit River.'

It was estimated that in 1928 some 150,000 cases of liquor a month, the vast majority of it Canadian whisky, crossed the Detroit river. Tougher controls reduced that to 50,000 cases in 1929. Many interested parties began shipping through the French territory of St Pierre and Miquelon off the Newfoundland coast, where the Bronfmans owned two businesses: the Atlas Shipping Co. and the Northern Export Company. These handled whiskies from 'Distillers Company-Seagrams Ltd Montreal, DCL of Edinburgh and from other European sources'.

Informed local opinion in Waterloo, Ontario, indicates that the Bronfmans' late 1920s stock-market takeover of the Seagram company gave them massive stocks of top-quality, mature whiskies that were ideal for American markets tired of inferior blends and concoctions.

In fact, when William Ross of the Scottish DCL Company inspected the Seagram, Waterloo, warehouses on 26 November 1929, with a view to joining in the purchase with the Bronfmans, he reported a stock of 6.3 million litres (1,664,328 US gallons).

getting canned Not an expression that came

about by chance. When the Bronfman family took control of Seagrams in 1928/9, one of their first innovations was to introduce tin cans of Canadian whisky that could easily be hidden under clothing. One brand was cheekily called Knickerbocker.

Captain William McCoy Otherwise known as 'the real McCoy', he negotiated a deal with Francis Berry of Berry Bros & Rudd, whisky suppliers to George V of Great Britain, in 1924. Using his notorious clipper, the *Arethusa*, and one other ship, Captain McCoy operated between the Bahamas and St Pierre and Miquelon. Initially he ran Caribbean rum, along 'rum runners row' between Boston and Atlantic City to longshore men who met him outside United States territorial waters.

In 1924 he changed to running Cutty Sark Scotch whisky, the first pale-coloured blend ever seen. When questioned about its unusual colour he is reported to have said: 'This whisky comes from the man who supplies King George V. I assure you it's the real McCoy.'

Cary A. Nation Under this assumed moniker, the elderly anti-alcohol crusader did much to further the cause of Prohibition. She was easily recognisable, with a fireman's axe in one hand and a Bible in the other. Four years after her death in 1911, an extensive moonshine operation was uncovered on her father's old farm in Missouri.

Minnesota 13 This was the contribution of Stearns County, Minnesota, to the production of moonshine. The name came from an anonymous gentleman distiller in Holdingford who produced a better-quality version. To guarantee that he had personally distilled the moonshine, he wrote his labels by hand, calling the whisky Minnesota 13. The *St Paul Dispatch* later wrote that it had, 'enough power to run a Great Northern freight from St Cloud to Fargo'. A federal officer told the same paper that he believed that in Minnesota 'there were about 1,200 stills boiling during Prohibition'.

Sweet Whiskey   In some cities in the mid-west a concoction called Sweet Whiskey was especially popular in speakeasies. Few could have been aware of its contents. It was generally produced by boiling a spirit of nitrous ether which included both nitric and sulphuric acids. Apparently it was not always gentle on the urinary organs.

'American Whiskey'   Whiskey of varying standards was produced in Mexico and smuggled in through San Diego, on the California/Mexico border, and El Paso in Texas. Mary Dowling, the first-ever woman distiller of Kentucky Bourbon was responsible for some good-quality ones. When Prohibition came into force she moved to Mexico and began to produce a Jim Beam look-alike. Others distillers used rotten cactus and potatoes to make the most basic spirits which masqueraded as whiskey.

the Windsor widow   This somewhat optimistic lady lived one block from the Detroit river in Windsor, Ontario. When she was arrested and brought before a court to explain her purchase of 40 cases and nine barrels of whisky over a six-month period, she explained to the magistrate that she had recently developed a drink problem and was consuming five bottles a day. On hearing her lucid defence, he found her guilty.

$100 or else   In Sonoma County, California, an abalone fisherman called Fred Barnes explained his involuntary initiation into the trade. Walking near Stewart's Point he noticed a suspicious line which led out to a launch and guessed that some whisky was about to be hauled in. At that moment he turned around and a 'guy stuck a gun' in his face and persuaded him to 'meet the boss' who made him an offer he couldn't refuse – to fill his Hudson Brougham 'full of White Horse Scotch from Canada' and deliver it to 'a man called Williams in the Sacramento Valley'.

the Enterprise   This saloon in Third Street, Sonoma, owned by Thomas Gemetti was a favourite haunt of judges and police officers. Somehow it escaped closure for the entire duration of Prohibition. Rumours suggested that four hours' notice was always given of any intended raid.

whisky in the sky   Prohibition was concurrent with the early development of commercial air travel and an unusual incident was reported in California in 1929. A new daily service was implemented from Santa Rosa to Oakland and then San Francisco. Local historian Gaye LeBaron recorded some 'hanky panky' surrounding the airline's owner, Al Bondi, and its sole pilot, Ted Peoples. In 1931 Ted was arrested. He had apparently been caught red-handed after landing on a small airstrip at Covelo and a not insubstantial consignment of contraband liquor was seized.

The trial was the event of the year. Many local stores closed and 500 people tried to cram their way into the Covelo courtroom to observe their hero being acquitted by the local jury, some of whom may not have been total abstainers.

Yack Yack Bourbon   This extremely dark liquor was produced from any kind of alcoholic spirit in Chicago speakeasies. It was flavoured and coloured with iodine, burnt sugar and a variety of other unsuitable substances. In 1923 the *Chicago Daily News* carried the story of a Southern visitor to the city who was charged $16 for a quart, of which he had drunk half. It quoted him as saying: 'I'm not feeling rational yet. I'm still uncertain and subject to fits.'

Was Prohibition worthwhile?   A 1936 poll by the American Institute of Public Opinion asked if conditions were better or worse after repeal. Thirty-six per cent said better, 33 per cent worse and 31 per cent indicated no change. In effect, the United States had turned many millions of law-abiding citizens into criminals.

American Whiskeys

California whiskey The first commercial operation was the Novelty distillery at the corner of Folsom and Price Streets in San Francisco. It dated from around 1850 and was destroyed by fire in 1855. An explosion within a copper cylinder resulted in two deaths and six other people were severely injured. A fireman called Thomas Seward was mortally wounded when a wall collapsed.

The four-storey distillery was operated by two men, Hirschfield and Barnett, and employed about 30 men. '45,000 gallons of whisky, 600 gallons of alcohol and about 10,000 bushels of grain were consumed' in the fire.

The latest California whiskey is Old Potrero produced by Anchor Distilling of San Francisco, a sister company of the Anchor Brewing Company. In 1996 it released a one-year-old single malt rye whiskey and will offer older styles as they become available.

Carolina whiskey In 1682 Thomas Ashe recorded that at Charleston in the Carolinas a beer was made from Indian corn and 'a strong spirit like brandy may be drawn off from it, by the help of an alembik [still]'.

Illinois   The state was an active whiskey producer with distilleries in Springfield and Peoria. One built in Peoria in the nineteenth century was mentioned by the writer Carl Sandburg in his autobiography. In the twentieth century Hiram Walker built one of the world's largest distilleries there.

Indiana   The House of Seagram produces whiskey on a large scale at Lawrenceburg. Seagram's Seven Crown is its principal brand there.

Maryland   The state once possessed the giant Calvert distillery at Relay but this has been demolished.

Minnesota   Because Minnesota had been so active during Prohibition, a company called Benz and Sons was encouraged to open a distillery in St Paul shortly after the 1933 repeal for the production of Wabash Valley Whisky.

Monongahela whiskey   This comes from the valley of that name, in Pennsylvania, and was the first whiskey to achieve a reputation in more than one state in the eighteenth century.

Ohio whiskey   In the middle of the nineteenth century Ohio was the second largest wine-producing state in the United States, so whiskey came second. However, some good rye was made, including that from the Hayner Distilling Co. founded in Dayton in 1866.

Pennsylvania pot still Bourbon   This is a great rarity, but any whiskey made to the Bourbon formula can carry the name, regardless of the state where it is produced. Today the most curious example is A.G. Hirsch Bourbon. It was distilled at Michter's distillery, apparently founded in 1753, near Shaefferstown, Pennsylvania. The distillery closed in 1988 but the Pennsylvania pot still Bourbon was bought from the remaining stock by a trader called Hirsch who, in a rather unorthodox manner, named it after himself. It is available at 16 or 20 years old and thousands of barrels are reported to be continuing to age and evaporate in the old distillery warehouses.

In the eighteenth and nineteenth centuries most Pennsylvania whiskeys were rye.

Tennessee   In many ways Tennessee has a similar geography and geology to Kentucky and, with its wealth of pure limestone water, the state was once the home of dozens of small distilleries. Only two have survived. The first is the world-renowned Jack Daniel's distillery at Lynchburg (see **Extremes**). It offers what must be the most entertaining visitor programme of any wine or drink producer on earth. An essential extra is a luncheon visit to Miss Mary Bobo's Boarding House where southern hospitality is dispensed with considerable charm by the delightful Lynne Tolley.

JACK DANIEL DISTILLERY
Lynchburg, Tennessee 37352;
tel: 615 759 6180;
fax: 615 759 6226.
Open 8.00 a.m – 4.00 p.m. every day except
Thanksgiving, Christmas, New Year's Day.

Its only competitor is George Dickel's Cascade distillery at Tullahoma with its fine ten-year-old whisky. Dickel was one of the very few Germans ever to own a whisky distillery. When asked why there is no e in whisky, the staff always blame 'old George who could never spell properly'.

GEORGE DICKEL'S CASCADE DISTILLERY
1950 Cascade Hollow Road,
Tullahoma, Tennessee 37388;
tel: 615 857 3124
Open 9.00 a.m. – 3.00 p.m. every day except
Thanksgiving, Christmas, New Year's Day.

Virginia   Despite having one of the longest histories as a whiskey-producing state, Virginia now only possesses the A. Smith Bowman distillery, at Fredericksburg, which is well known for its Virginia Gentleman Bourbon, a great favourite in Washington, DC.

Canadian Whiskies

Whisky production was initially the sole domain of small farmers – many of Scottish and Irish origin with pot stills. Following Henry Hudson's 1610 voyage, both British and French settlers arrived in Canada and as early as 1643 distillation was on a sufficient scale for the British authorities to prohibit the sale of whisky to Indians.

During the eighteenth century many immigrants settled in the American and Canadian colonies and often constructed stills without delay. Ken Desson and Norman Bell wrote in *Canadian Heritage* that, 'Distilleries sprang up in most British North American towns with a population of more than 500 people.' Later, following the American War of Independence, thousands of British loyalists, many from whisky-producing areas, headed north and re-settled in what became known, in 1791, as Upper Canada (Ontario) and Lower Canada (Quebec).

Early distillation in Canada differed little from that in the United States. However, in 1794 events took a different turn when the British government, having been ejected from America, demonstrated its authority in Canada by imposing the first tax on stills. A charge of one shilling and threepence a gallon provided Upper Canada's main source of revenue for the next half-century.

Many small operators disappeared as a result of the tax and the development of larger distilleries attached to local grist mills began. The floors of the mills provided plenty of unused husks and middlings, which were mashed together ensuring that nothing went to waste. The quality of much of the early whisky had been relatively poor, and the large-scale distillers created growing competition and a vast improvement in standards. In 1799 John Molson constructed a distillery and a brewery in Montreal, and between 1820 and 1867 the family may well have been the largest distillers in North America. In 1821 they were the first to export Canadian whisky to Great Britain but in 1867, probably as a result of the growing temperance movement and the increasing exportation of other whiskies, they dramatically closed their great Montreal distillery and concentrated on beer. The company is still a major international influence in this market today.

The two greatest Canadian whisky influences had just begun to flex their muscles in the mid-nineteenth century. Joseph E. Seagram was a rising employee at the Waterloo distillery, and American citizen Hiram Walker had moved to Windsor, Ontario, where he was busily developing his unique Walkerville. They were to make Canadian whisky famous throughout the world.

Today there are 13 distilleries in Canada. Most of the whisky is made from corn, rye and barley. Corn provides about 85 per cent of production, with only Alberta Distillers in Calgary concentrating on rye.

The actual composition of Canadian whisky is generally somewhat different from that of other countries. The normal pattern is to make a light-flavoured base whisky from corn (maize), to which a fuller-bodied style, usually made from rye (and occasionally from barley), is added to give more flavour. The whisky has a minimum ageing requirement of three years but most premium brands are over four years old.

Canadian whisky's largest piece of good fortune was American Prohibition. As an industry it had been suffering from sales of Scotch whisky. Before the Volstead Act its success in the United States had been relatively limited, but with the closure, or mothballing, of American distilleries the Canadians enjoyed a golden era. They were not concerned about United States laws. If American citizens wanted to enjoy Canadian whisky that was fine, as long as somebody paid for it somewhere along the line. As a result, Americans became familiar with the light, smooth flavour of many Canadian whiskies, which contrasted with that of fuller-flavoured Bourbons, and their popularity has helped to maintain a giant market to this day.

Among the most popular Canadian whiskies

are: Adams Private Stock, Alberta Premium, Black Velvet, Canadian Mist, Canadian Tradition, Gibson's Finest, Hiram Walker Canadian Club, Hiram Walker Northern Light, Melcher's Very Mild, McGuinness Silk Tassel, Potter's Special Old Premium, Schenley Golden Wedding, Seagram's VO, Seagram's Crown Royal, Windsor Canadian and Wiser's Old.

English and Welsh Whiskies

The Bristol Distillery   This is believed to have been founded in the seventeenth century at Cheese Lane alongside Bristol harbour. The earliest documentation concerning the whisky is dated 1761. Property records show that in 1821 it was owned by Thomas Castle & Co. In 1830 it was transferred to Thomas Harris & Co, and in 1863 was purchased by Joseph Thomas Board and his family, who incorporated it as the Bristol Distilling Co. Ltd. An 1828 Ashmead map shows a large barley field adjacent to the south side of Cheese Lane. In 1887 the distillery had 100 employees and used three pot stills with capacities of 10,000, 7000 and 6000 gallons (45,400, 31,900 and 27,300 litres) and also had patent stills for the production of grain spirit. In about 1920 the company was taken over by DCL, itself later acquired by United Distillers.

In 1825 Bristol had four other small distilleries. They made a variety of alcoholic drinks but it is not known if any of them produced whiskies.

Lake District whisky   The illicit distillation of whisky was quite widespread in Cumberland and Westmoreland during the nineteenth century. The best-known character was Lancelot (Lanty) Slee (1802–76), who combined three jobs for most of his life: quarryman, farmer and distiller. He lived on a small farm at Low Arnside near Ambleside. His son Adam, born when his father was 63, recalled when he was 100 years old that, 'he used to make the best stuff out of sour beer and he charged about 10 shillings a gallon for it'.

Lanty operated four or five different stills at a time. Their sites included a cave at Bessycrag quarry in the Wetherlan foothills, another at Hall Garth, a second quarry at Atkinson Coppice, a stable at the foot of Tilberthwaite Gill and a hiding-place below the kitchen of his farm. He was arrested on several occasions, imprisoned at least twice and fined £100 at Ambleside in 1853.

Moses Rigg, a contemporary of Lanty Slee, was another prominent illicit distiller. The early rock-climber George Graham (1872–1963) described how Moses had constructed a stone hut on Gable Crag on the face of Great Gable, which was said to be the highest building in England. He explained how it had a still and Moses 'used bog water'. Although the hut's position was known, the view was so open that Moses and his friend Dan Tyson would have had plenty of time to escape if the need had arisen.

Lancashire   The county has a lengthy history of whisky production, both legal and illicit. Its earliest record comes from the listing of a 'bake to distil waters' in the 1557 will of Richard Brereton de Ley of Brereton.

In 1761 Robert Preston founded the Vauxhall distillery in Liverpool which, at its peak, employed around 150 people. Over a hundred years later Alfred Barnard described it as the 'largest distillers in the kingdom'. It continued until early in the twentieth century. Liverpool was also home to the Bank Hall distillery; also owned by the Preston family, it was prominent in the nineteenth century. In 1814 Liverpool possessed seven more distilleries: Bishop's, Robert Greenham & Co., Holgrave's, King & Co., Miller's, Seddon & Co., and Jeremiah Steel. However, it is not certain that all were involved in whisky production.

In 1824 Manchester had six distilleries under the names Collier, Duckworth, Fowler, Milne, Newall, and William Willet & Sons. In 1849 nearby Bolton had a distillery called Hall's in Nelson Square.

In 1991 there was a glimmer of hope when Lancashire Whisky Producers Ltd was formed at Wigan. Although it does not have a distillery it buys new spirit from 'a confidential source' and ages and blends it in Lancashire. Marketed as Red Rose, it is stocked by a growing number of specialists.

Illicit whisky producers took advantage of

Lancashire's peat moors and damp climate during the eighteenth and nineteenth centuries. Lancashire Whisky Producers Ltd says, 'Between 1835 and 1837 no less than 21 illegal distilleries were found in Bolton alone.' There is also the 1858 tale of the Blackburn brewer Daniel Thwaite, whose brewery still thrives today. He was a justice of the peace and fined James Morris of Pike Lowe £230 for avoiding the payment of revenue. Although it was then an enormous sum, it seems small compared to the estimated excise loss of £700 per annum for over 50 years. Morris was forced to sell his property in order to pay the fine.

Illicit distillation became such a problem that from 1838 to 1848 an excise officer operated from Haslingden. He was eventually withdrawn because the distillers, known locally as 'whisky-spinners', were too clever for him. One method of transporting whisky involved the use of hollow metal saddles concealed beneath cloth covers on donkeys.

London   Although London was better known for gin distilleries the Lea Valley distillery, owned by E. A. Brock was active at Stratford in the East End during the second half of the nineteenth century. Another distillery is believed to have operated at Thamesmead near Woolwich.

Welsh whisky   This is a fascinating, if limited, story and it seems certain that there must be other evidence waiting to be unearthed.

Welsh legend, passed down orally over 700 years before it was committed to paper, tells of Reallt Hir, a Celtic chieftain who made a strong clear liquor from a barley beer on Bardsey Island in about 356 AD. The legend suggests that the Celts learnt the art of distillation from Greek sailors. It is, of course, unprovable but not impossible.

The modern story of Welsh whisky appears to originate in Dale, Pembrokeshire, where a family called Williams abandoned their whisky distillery in 1707 and emigrated to Prince William County, Virginia. Their grandson, Evan Williams, was to erect Kentucky's first purpose-built commercial distillery in 1783.

Somewhat later, in the nineteenth century, there was the short-lived but colourful episode of the Welsh Whisky Distillery at Frongoch, near Bala in North Wales. (See **Lloyd Price, Richard John: Colourful Characters**)

The next development in the story of Welsh whisky came in 1974, when Dafydd Gittins and Mal Morgan acquired an old pub in Brecon, with a tiny, moribund brewery attached. There they experimented in compounding whisky with herbs and spices in a manner similar to many old recipes for *usquebaugh*. The partnership was dissolved but Daydd continued independently, rejecting offers of financial help and battling on alone. He bought Scotch malt whisky and grain spirit and blended them in Brecon, and in 1992 the Welsh Whisky Company distilled its first pure Welsh single malt. The stocky former Brecon rugby star suffered many unkind taunts over the years, but his future looks bright with his Welsh whiskies Swn-y-Mor and Prince of Wales in demand in several countries.

Irish Whiskeys

Long before Scotch whisky evolved, Irish whiskey production was an active industry with a unique history. Legends tell of Irish monks who travelled to the Mediterranean in about the sixth century and returned with the secret of distillation.

Production burgeoned from 1750 onwards and in 1779 a record 1152 distilleries were registered. Unfortunately, in the same year, an act of Parliament imposed strictures which saw the numbers drop so dramatically that by 1796 just 214 distilleries were officially in operation. The government actively encouraged fewer, larger, distilleries in the belief that the industry would be easier to supervise. The official figure for whiskey production in 1806 was 11,400,000 gallons (51,800,000 litres) roughly one-third of the previous peak figure. By 1821 the total of registered distilleries had dwindled to just 32!

But Ireland was already looking overseas for trade: on 11 October 1817 the *Lexington Gazette* in Kentucky ran an advertisement for an un-named Irish whiskey available from a local firm called Kentucky Grocers.

The nineteenth century saw the proliferation of brand names and a consistency of quality that had previously been unknown. In 1887, when Alfred Barnard wrote his *Whisky Distilleries of the United Kingdom*, he listed 28 Irish distilleries (although he overlooked some). Whiskey production had become a major export business but soon all that was going to change. The introduction of Scotch blended whisky (see **Aeneas Coffey: The Excise Man**) wreaked havoc on the sales of Irish pot still whiskey which was heavier in character. Much has been written about Irish whiskey always being triple-distilled, but in the last century this was the exception rather than the rule.

In 1966 all the remaining whiskey producers in the Republic of Ireland merged to form Irish Distillers, nowadays owned by Pernod Ricard. The little Bushmills distillery from Northern Ireland joined them six years later. Irish Distillers concentrated on only three distilleries: Bushmills; the Midleton, which was entirely modernised; and the old Jameson's Bow Street premises in Dublin, where only the warehouse operation was retained. The group also implemented a policy of triple distillation and, with the exception of Paddy, always used the e.

In 1989 the new Cooley distillery brought excitement back to Irish whiskey which had been in retreat for so long. It began making both pot still and blended whiskeys of flavour and character at Dundalk in the Republic of Ireland while ageing them in the old Locke's distillery at Kilbeggan. This may be opened at some later stage.

In 1994 Irish Distillers licensed Tullamore Dew to Allied Domecq, who later passed control to C. & C. International of Dublin, makers of Irish Mist liqueur. However, the production of Tullamore Dew (see **Intriguing Stories**) has continued without interruption at the Midleton distillery.

Irish whiskey visits
VW = visitors welcome
VA = visitors by appointment

THE BUSHMILLS DISTILLERY
Bushmills, Co. Antrim, N. Ireland;
tel: 01265 731521. VW

IRISH WHISKEY CORNER
Bow Street, Dublin;
tel: 01872 5566. VW

THE JAMESON HERITAGE CENTRE
Midleton Distillery, Midleton, Co. Cork;
tel: 021 613594. VW

LOCKE'S DISTILLERY MUSEUM
Kilbeggan, Co. Westmeath;
Tel: 0506 32134. VA

Irish whiskies currently available
Avoca blended

Black Bush Premium Blend
Bow Street 27 year old, Cadenhead's (single
  distillery blend)
Bushmills Blended
Bushmills 5-year and 10-year-old Single Malt
Bushmills 12-year-old De-Luxe Blend 1608 (duty-
  free only)
Bushmills Millennium 25 year old.

Coleraine Blend (from Bushmills)
Connemara Single Malt (peated)
Dunphy's Blend from Midleton
Green Spot Pot Still (produced by Jameson's for
  Mitchell & Son of Dublin)
Hewitt's Blend from Midleton
Inishowen Peated Blend from Cooley Distillers
Jameson's Blend
Jameson's 1780 De-Luxe 12 year old
Jameson's Distillery Reserve 12 year old (some
  sherry ageing)
Jameson's Crested Ten
John's Lane 34 year old, Cadenhead's (single
  distillery blend)
John Locke's Premium Blend (Cooley Distillers)
John Power & Son Blend (from Midleton)
Kilbeggan Blended

Midleton Very Rare Limited Edition Annual
   Distillation (Blend)
Millar's Black Label
Mulligan's Liqueur
Murphy's
Paddy Blend from Midleton
Redbreast 12-year-old pot-still malt from
   Jameson's
Royal Irish 39-year-old single malt, Cadenhead's
Tullamore Dew Blend from Midleton
Tyrconnell Single Malt

Some of these are difficult to find; see **Whisky
   Specialists**.

Kentucky Bourbon Whiskeys

Romantic history suggests that the first Kentuckians, inspired by tales of Daniel Boone's hunting expeditions to the western extremes of Virginia, packed up their belongings and crossed the Appallachian mountains in search of paradise. Whiskey legends hint that among them were the first Kentucky distillers, mainly disgruntled Scots–Irish (Ulster) immigrants who had made whiskey in Pennsylvania but left in their droves following the 1791 whiskey tax and ensuing riots. These accounts are not supported by fact: records for 1810 show that Pennsylvania was still producing around three times more whiskey than Kentucky.

The Scots–Irish legend can also be largely refuted by examining the names of the earliest Kentucky distillers. For example, when the *Nelson County Record* published a special edition in 1896 to celebrate the county's centenary, it listed the original distillers. Among them was the odd Mackenna, McClaskey and McGee, but there were far more names from England or Wales – Mattingley, Moore, Hart, Hayden, Weller, Clark, Parker, Ford, Bowling and Price – not to mention Boehm (later Beam) from Germany and Drillette from France.

It is impossible to say who the first farmer-distiller was as no official records were made at the time. It must have been the first man to arrive in the future state with his own still and put it to work. However, he may have used any wild fruits in the vicinity rather than distilling whisky. Among the very earliest farmer-distillers of whiskey were John Ritchie, Wattie Boone, Stephen Ritchie, Jacob Meyers and the Davis brothers, Joseph and Samuel. The term 'farmer-distiller' indicates a man who farmed several mixed crops including rye and corn and made whiskey from them.

No account of Kentucky Bourbon would be complete without the Reverend Elijah Craig. Long-standing Kentucky folklore credits him with the accidental birth of Bourbon through using charred barrels and so discovering the beneficial charring of oak. He was a part-time Baptist pastor and farmer-distiller who arrived in Scott County in 1785. It was reported that in 1789 he had an outhouse fire which resulted in some barrels being undamaged and others charred.

When he next made whiskey the run was of sufficient volume to require the use of all the casks. Understandably, the whiskey from the clean barrels was consumed first and this meant the remainder aged longer in the charred casks and took on the colour of the charcoal. It was also found to be smoother.

Recently some Kentucky distillers have wondered why the casks were charred only on the inside and not all over. However, if they had held whiskey previously they would have been impregnated with the alcohol and expert coopers say that the likely result is that the interiors of the barrels would catch fire before their exteriors. If Craig was indeed the first to use charred barrels, we can be sure that he did not make anything like the fine, mature Kentucky Bourbons of today.

The known facts are that Elijah Craig was a pioneer Kentucky whiskey distiller who personally took flat boats down to New Orleans. On one occasion, he, along with others, was fined for operating a still without a licence.

There is plenty of argument about the original naming of Bourbon, but in all probability it came about in the following way. When the first settlers moved westwards they found pure, sweet, limestone water and soil that could provide corn (maize) and rye in profusion. Barley was introduced a little later. Many settlers carried their own stills and soon began producing pot-still whiskeys for very local consumption. Great numbers settled in the large fertile region that was officially named Bourbon County, Virginia, in 1786. The choice of name was an acknowledgement of the support the French had given to the American colonies in their fight for independence. The state of Kentucky was officially founded in 1792 and included Bourbon County, which became one of the most prolific areas for whiskey production.

The first specific export trade developed with whiskies being shipped, on flat boats, down small local tributaries to the Ohio river and then into the Mississippi. Kentucky whiskeys entered Spanish America on that giant waterway and drifted down to the Louisiana ports of Natches and New Orleans. Consignments arrived there from numerous towns and villages in states like the Carolinas, Tennessee, Virginia, West Virginia and Kentucky itself. Within a short space of time the whiskeys from Bourbon County became favoured and the word was on the barrels themselves. It should be remembered that Louisiana had belonged to Spain since 1762 and identifying some of the best whiskeys with a royal name must have appealed to buyers. It is likely that these first exported whiskies were made only from rye.

Whiskey historian Michael Veach recorded that, 'in 1780 John Ritchie had made enough surplus whiskey to fill a flat boat that he sailed down the river to New Orleans to sell'. This appears to be the first instance of an evolving type of exportation when both whiskey and boats were sold. Many farmer-distillers re-invested a large part of the proceeds in horses, and spent months walking them back to their farms. In doing so they founded the Kentucky horse-breeding industry.

In 1783 Evan Williams built his Kentucky whiskey distillery in Ohio Falls, now Louisville (see **Colourful Characters**).

It was a couple more generations before Kentucky whiskey became a really serious commercial business in its own right. In the meantime, the identification of Bourbon began to develop. In 1821 Stout and Adams at Maysville, Kentucky, placed the first-ever advertisement for Bourbon Whiskey by the barrel. Unfortunately, they did not define the description any further.

In 1833 a Lexington distillery belonging to Daniel and Henry McCocran offered to purchase corn, rye and barley – the three traditional cereals that are nowadays a legal requirement for Bourbon.

In 1863 the New York City grocer Bininger's, who had sold the first bottles of Bourbon in 1849, proudly announced their offer of an Old Kentucky Bourbon identified as 'Bininger's 1863 Reserve being distilled in 1862'. The advertising poster proudly claimed that it was, 'peculiarly effective for the treatment of lung complaints, dyspepsia, derangement's of the stomach, nervousness, etc.'

In 1870 the first Kentucky Bourbon was bottled and marketed as a brand. It was Old Forrester (later it lost an *r*) and was the brainchild of George Brown, who later founded Brown Forman. It was said to have been named after a Dr Forrester of Louisville, who had asked if someone could provide a Bourbon of a consistent quality for medical prescriptions.

It was the first of many medicinal whiskeys and the precedent it set was to prove useful during Prohibition, when six adroit Kentucky distilleries suddenly realised the increasing needs of an ailing population. On 19 November 1929 they were given the authority to proceed with the joint operation of The American Medicinal Liquor Co. with permission to distribute 5,291,106 litres (1,397,800 US gallons) a year for health purposes – enough to relieve 12 million influenza victims.

Prohibition exacted an alarming toll on the Kentucky Bourbon industry and in the late 1970s and early 1980s the decline in the popularity of spirits in the United States brought matters to an all-time low. But the entrepreneurial spirit that had originally helped to establish Kentucky and its Bourbon found new vigour. Bourbon began to sell itself around the world and the later rise of single-barrel and other speciality Bourbons attracted new respect in America.

1996 even saw a revival of pot-still Kentucky Bourbon with Brown Forman's introduction of Woodford Reserve, produced at the old Labrot & Graham distillery in Woodford County – a much-awaited delight that should be ready around 2002 or 2003.

Today, for a whiskey to be called Bourbon, United States federal law requires that its mash must consist of not less than 51 per cent corn (maize), plus rye or wheat and malted barley. It must be aged for a minimum of two years and no colouring or flavouring must be added.

In January 1997 ten distilleries were operating in Kentucky.

VW = visitors welcome
NV = no visitors
VA = visitors by appointment

THE EARLY TIMES DISTILLERY
850 Dixie Highway, Louisville, Kentucky 40201;
tel: 502 585 1100
Brands: Early Times, Old Forester. VA.

THE BERNHEIM DISTILLERY
1701 West Breckinridge, Louisville,
Kentucky 40210;
tel: 502 585 9100
Brands: I.W. Harper, James E. Pepper, Kentucky Tavern, Old Charter, Old Fitzgerald, W.L. Weller, Rebel Yell. NV.

THE JIM BEAM DISTILLERY
Clermont, Kentucky 40110;
tel: 502 543 9877
Brands: Jim Beam in various styles, Booker's, Baker's, Basil Hayden's, Old Taylor, Knob Creek, Old Grand-Dad, Old Crow. VW but restricted to Jim Beam's American outpost with two museums, a warehouse, a shop and a video of the distillery.

THE ANCIENT AGE DISTILLERY
1001 Wilkinson Boulevard, Frankfort,
Kentucky 40601;
tel: 502 223 7641. Open 9.00 a.m. – 2.00 p.m.
Monday to Friday groups by appointment.
Brands: Ancient Age, Blanton's, Rock Hill Farms,
Elmer T. Lee, Hancock's Reserve, Benchmark XO,
Eagle Rare.

MAKER'S MARK DISTILLERY
Loretto, Kentucky 40037;
tel: 502 865 2099. Monday to Saturday, Sunday
afternoons.
Brands: Maker's Mark. VW

WILD TURKEY DISTILLERY
Highway 1510, Lawrenceburg, Kentucky 40342;
tel: 502 839 4544. Four 75-minute tours Monday
to Friday, closed last 2 weeks July, first week
January; groups by appointment.
Brands: Wild Turkey, Wild Turkey Kentucky Spirit,
Wild Turkey Rare Breed.

FOUR ROSES DISTILLERY
1224 Bonds Hill Road, Lawrenceburg,
Kentucky 40342;
tel: 502 839 3436
Brands: Four Roses (Export only). VA.

HEAVEN HILL DISTILLERY
Loretto Road, Bardstown, Kentucky 40004;
tel: 502 348 3921
Brands: Heaven Hill, Evan Williams, Elijah Craig,
J.W. Dant, J.T.S. Brown, Mattingley & Moore,
Henry McKenna. Visitors advised to phone in
advance.

PO Box 788, Bardstown, Kentucky 40004.
tel: 502 348 3991; Fax: 502 348 0231. VA.
Brands: Very Old Barton, Tom Moore, Barclays,
Colonel Lee, Kentucky Gentleman, Ten High.

7855 McCracken Pike, Versailles, Kentucky 40383.
tel: 606 879 1812; Fax: 606 879 1947. VA.
Brands: Woodford Reserve.

Bardstown is the 'Bourbon Capital of the World'
and houses the American Whiskey Museum (see
Museums) as well as having two distilleries. It
hosts the annual Kentucky Bourbon Festival and
provides a wide range of folksy restaurants. The
Tourist & Convention Commission, PO Box 867B,
Bardstown, Kentucky 40004, tel: 1 800 638 4877
is a fund of information.

Scotch Single Malt Whiskies

Ages given for malts were accurate at the time of writing but will vary as stocks are depleted and casks replaced. Regard them as an indication of likely availability.

This list attempts to identify all distilleries that are active, mothballed, closed and even those which have been demolished, but whose malts can still be bought from specialists.

In the middle of the nineteenth century most of the Scotch whisky sold was single malt but usually of a young age. Then the rise of blended whiskies saw the consumption of malts decline dramatically. By the early twentieth century sales were largely confined to specialist suppliers.

Blends continued to grow in popularity and malts largely disappeared until in 1969. The Glenfiddich began marketing itself as a single malt. A new era was born in which serious enthusiasts began to analyse and compare the malts from many different distilleries.

Regions   There is much debate on this topic. The regions below have been selected on the advice of a number of experienced Scotch whisky producers.

Lowlands   Traditionally a region where many malt distilleries once used triple distillation to make light, elegant whiskies. Sadly, only two out of eight malts available in bottle are still in active production: Auchentoshan near Glasgow and Glenkinchie near Edinburgh.

Campbeltown   At its peak in the last century Campbeltown could boast some 33 distilleries. Today only two malts, Springbank and Longrow, both from the same distillery, are made. Sheltered on the inland shore of the Mull of Kintyre, this region supplied many mid- to full-flavoured, often slightly sweet, whiskies that varied considerably in quality. The survivors remain proud flag bearers.

Islay   Paradise for lovers of pungent, peaty drams, it is an island where the sea sweeps in as the seasons change in the course of a day. Brine, peat, ancient rocks and unique water contribute to some of the greatest whiskies on earth. The island's eight malts vary in depth of flavour from Bruichladdich, the lightest, to Bowmore in the middle, to the most powerful, Laphroaig.

Islands   (This is a geographical term and there is considerable variety of styles.) It is difficult to justify one region for malts that come from different islands and varying climates. For all practical purposes the Islands region is a collection of individual jewels. Perhaps each island deserves its own region.

Highland   The largest of all regions and many whisky books include Speyside within it. But surely Speyside produces so many fine, rich, smooth malts that it should be entitled to its own denomination.

Speyside   The most prolific of regions and home of more world-famous single malts than any other area. Somehow the match of climate, soils and water marry together with the most consistent results.

For part of the nineteenth century Glenlivet was one of the five official regions and at various times as many as 29 malts have been entitled to add Glenlivet to their distillery name. This arose following a court case in 1880 when *The* Glenlivet sued other distilleries using the name. The ruling permitted other malts to use a hyphen before the name, either because they stood within the Glen, or valley of the Livet river, or because they made malt whisky in the same style. In this chapter these are identified by the use of -Glenlivet, which many do not use. *The* Glenlivet, which is one of the best-known malts, is listed in its own right and there is only one of its name.

To help the reader the following abbreviations have been used to indicate visiting facilities at distilleries.

VW = visitors welcome

NV = no visitors

VA = visitors by appointment only

The writer does not pretend to have tasted each whisky listed and has sought help with descriptions. Many tasting notes come from the distilleries' own information, some from helpful fellow professionals and others from personal tasting. Tasting notes for a few whiskies have not been given either because they are not yet old enough for release, or due to extreme scarcity.

Stockists are given for each entry. For full details of specialist whisky suppliers, see pages 141–3.

Lowlands

AUCHENTOSHAN
Dalmuir, Dunbartonshire.
Founded 1823. Owned by Morrison Bowmore. Triple-distilled (see **Extremes**) 10 and 15 year old available from Cadenhead's, no age and 1972 from Gordon & MacPhail. Most elegant of all, light, charming and soft, slight sweetness.
Source: Kilpatrick Hills Springs. NV.

BLADNOCH
Bladnoch, Wigtownshire DG8 9AB.
Founded 1817, now closed. Owned by United Distillers. Available as 10 year old in Flora and Fauna series and 16 and 28 year old from Cadenhead's, and 1984 and '85 from Gordon & MacPhail. Elegant nose but quite full flavour for Lowland.
Source: Loch Ma Berry.

GLENKINCHIE
Pencaitland, Tranent, East Lothian EH34 5ET; tel: 01875 340333.
Founded c. 1837. Owned by United Distillers. Available at 10 years. Soft aromatic nose, light-medium palate, smooth dry finish.
Source: Lammermuir Hills. VW.

INVERLEVEN
Dumbarton, Dunbartonshire.
Founded 1938, now closed. Owned by Allied Distillers. Available as 1984 from Gordon & MacPhail. Slightly smoky nose, fullish, quite smooth.
Source: Loch Lomond.

KINCLAITH
Moffat Street, Glasgow.
Founded 1957, demolished 1976. Available as 26 year old in the Whisky Shop, Lincoln.

LITTLE MILL
Bowling, Dunbartonshire, now mothballed.
Owned by Gibson International. Available as 8 year old from Gordon & MacPhail. Elegant nose, soft and mellow.
Source: Kilpatrick Springs.

ROSEBANK
Camelon, Falkirk, Stirlingshire.
Founded 1840, now closed. Owned by United Distillers. Available as 12 year old and 1984 from Gordon & MacPhail and in Flora and Fauna series. Light bouquet, well balanced, dry.
Source: Carron Valley Reservoir.

ST MAGDALENE
Linlithgow, West Lothian.
Founded 1798, now closed. Available as 1966 in Connoisseurs Choice and 1966 from Gordon & MacPhail and 14 year old from Cadenhead's. Light smoke on nose, quite full, sweet.
Source: Loch Lomond.

Campbeltown

GLEN SCOTIA
Campbeltown, Argyllshire.
Founded 1832, now mothballed. Owned by Loch
Lomond Distillery Co. Ltd. Available as 12 and 14
years from Gordon & MacPhail. Aromatic, big,
peaty malt with smooth body.
Source: Campbeltown Loch.

LONGROW
Springbank Distillery, Campbeltown, Argyllshire
PA28 6ET.
Founded 1824. Owned by J & A Mitchell & Co.
Ltd. Available as 17 and 21 years. Pungent aroma,
full mouthful with a hint of sweetness. NB: Not
triple-distilled as stated elsewhere. Own maltings.
Source: Crosshill Loch. VA.

SPRINGBANK
Campbeltown, Argyllshire PA28 6ET;
tel: 01586 552085.
Founded c. 1828. Owned by J & A Mitchell & Co.
Ltd. Available as 12, 15, 21, 25 and 30 years and

as 9 year old from Cadenhead's. Only un-chill-filtered malt. Own maltings. Benchmark dram, beautifully balanced, delightful finish. NB: Not triple-distilled as stated elsewhere. Own maltings. Source: Crosshill Loch. VA.

Islay

ARDBEG
Nr Port Ellen, Islay.
Founded 1794. Owned by Glenmorangie PLC. Available in Connoisseurs Choice and as 21 year old from Cadenhead's. Arguably most aromatic and pungent of all.
Source: Loch Arinambeast and Loch Uigedale. NV.

BOWMORE
Bowmore, Island of Islay, Argyllshire; tel: 01496 81441.
Founded 1779. Owned by Torii family of Japan. Available as Legend (no age given), 10, 12, 15, 17, 21, 25, 30 years and special bottlings. (See **Extremes**.) Own maltings, medium-peated, beautifully balanced, lingering finish.
Source: Laggan river. VW.

BRUICHLADDICH

Bruichladdich, Island of Islay, Argyllshire. Founded 1881, now mothballed. Owned by Whyte & Mackay. Available as 10, 15 and 21 year old and Stillman's Dram (approx. 25 years old), 17 year old from Cadenhead's and 1964 from Gordon & MacPhail. Lightest from Islay, dry and crisp.
Source: Hills behind distillery.

BUNNAHABHAIN

Port Askaig, Island of Islay, Argyllshire; tel: 01496 840646.
Founded 1881. Owned by Highland Distilleries Company Ltd. Available as 12 and 25 years, distilled 1964 from Matthew Gloag and Sons. Lightly peated for Islay, pleasant finish.
Source: Springs adjacent to distillery. VW.

CAOL ILA

Port Askaig, Island of Islay, Argyllshire; tel: 01496 840207.
Founded 1846. Owned by United Distillers. Available as 15 year old in Flora and Fauna series and 22 year old from Cadenhead's and 1981 from Gordon & MacPhail. Dry, quite peaty, good body.
Source: Loch Nam Ban. VW.

LAGAVULIN

Port Ellen, Island of Islay, Argyllshire; tel: 01496 302400.
Founded c. 1816. Owned by United Distillers. Available as 16 years. Aromatic nose, very big, full-flavoured mouthfull.
Source: Solan Lochs. VA.

LAPHROAIG

Port Ellen Island of Islay, Argyllshire;
tel: 01496 302418.
Founded 1821. Available as 10, 12 and 15 year
old from Cadenhead's. Remarkably aromatic
nose, full-flavoured bouquet, giant mouthful. Own
maltings.
Source: Kilbride river. VA.

PORT ELLEN

Port Ellen, Island of Islay, Argyllshire. Founded
1825, now closed. Available as 12 years (56.7
per cent) from Cadenhead's and 1979 and '80
from Gordon & MacPhail. Slightly aromatic peaty
mouthful. Own maltings.
Source: Leorin Lochs.

Islands

GLEN ROSA

Lochranza, Isle of Arran.
Newest distillery in Scotland. Opened 1995.
Estimated available 2005. NV.

HIGHLAND PARK

Kirkwall, Orkney;
tel: 01856 874619.
Founded 1795. Available as 8 and 12 year old and
1984 (58.6 per cent) from Gordon & MacPhail
and 18 year old from Cadenhead's. Smoky, peaty
nose, delicious palate, excellent balance. Own
maltings. Source: Cattie Maggie's Spring. VW.

ISLE OF JURA

Craighouse, Jura, Argyllshire;
tel: 01496 820240.
Founded 1810. Owned Whyte & Mackay.

Available as 10 and 11 year old from Cadenhead's and 27 years from Gordon & MacPhail. Fresh clean malt, pleasing light aroma.
Source: Market Loch. VA.

TOBERMORY
Ledaig distillery, Tobermory, Mull, Argyllshire; tel: 01688 302645.
Founded 1823. Owned by Burn Stewart. Available non-aged lightly peated Tobermory and highly peated Ledaig, as over 20 years Vintage from owners, 23 year old from Cadenhead's and 1974 from Gordon & MacPhail. Clean, fresh, elegant, dry palate. NB There is also a Tobermory label for a vatted malt. Source: Mishnish lochs. VW Easter–September.

SCAPA
Kirkwall Orkney KW15 1SE; tel: 01856 872071.
Founded 1885. Owned by Allied Distillers. Available as 1985 from Gordon & MacPhail and 8 year old from Cadenhead's. Delicious peaty nose, middleweight body, very smooth finish.
Source: Lingro Burn. VA.

TALISKER
Carbost, Isle of Skye,
Inverness-shire IV47 8SR;
tel: 01478 42203.
Founded 1831. Owned by United Distillers. Available at 10 years at an unusual strength of 45.8 per cent and 17 from Cadenhead's and 1955 from Gordon & MacPhail. Aromatic nose, delicious full flavour, slightly sweet.
Source: Cnoc-nan-Speireag. VW.

Highland

ABERFELDY

Aberfeldy, Perthshire PH5 2EB;
tel: 01887 820330.
Founded 1830. Owned by United Distillers.
Available as 15 year old in Flora and Fauna series,
17 from Cadenhead's and 1977 from Gordon &
MacPhail. Lightly peated, good body.
Source: Pitilie Burn. VW.

ARDMORE

Kennethmont, Aberdeenshire;
tel: 01464 3213.
Founded 1898. Owned by Allied Distillers.
Available as 17 years from Cadenhead's and 1981
from Gordon & MacPhail. Sweet, full-flavoured
malt.
Source: Several springs from Knockandy Hill. VA.

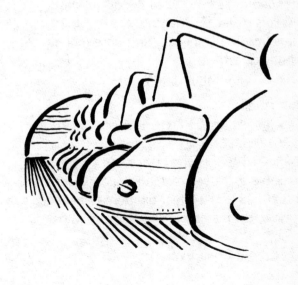

BALBLAIR

Edderton, Tain, Ross-shire;
tel: 01862 821273.
Founded 1790. Purchased in 1996 by Inver House Distillers. Available as 10 year old from Gordon & MacPhail and 26 from Cadenhead's. Attractive smokiness, slightly sweet.
Source: Struie Hill. VA.

BANFF

Banff, Banffshire.
Founded 1863, demolished 1983. Limited availability as 1974 from Gordon & MacPhail and in Connoisseurs Choice. Slightly smoky nose, firm mouthful.

BEN NEVIS

Fort William, Inverness-shire, PH33 6TJ;
tel: 01397 700200.
Founded c. 1825. Owned by Nikka Whisky Distillers of Japan. Available as 18, 19, 25 and 26 years from Cadenhead's. Rich nose, full palate, slightly sweet.
Source: Allt a Mhullin. VW.

BLAIR ATHOL

Pitlochry, Perthshire PH16 5LY;
tel: 01796 472234.
Founded 1798. Owned by United Distillers. Available as 12 year old in Flora and Fauna series and 20, 23 and 24 year old from Cadenhead's. Mellow, deep aroma, fruity flavours with smooth finish.
Source: Allt Dour. VW.

CLYNELISH (SOMETIMES KNOWN AS **BRORA**)
Brora, Sutherland KW9 6LR;
tel: 01408 621444.
Founded 1819. Owned by United Distillers.
Available as 14 years in Flora and Fauna series
and 13 year old from Cadenhead's and 1972 from
Gordon & MacPhail. Dry, fullish, medium peat.
Source: Clynmilton Burn. VW.

DALMORE
Alness, Ross-shire;
tel: 01349 882362.
Founded 1839. Owned by White & Mackay.
Available as 12 year old and as 19 and 30 from
Cadenhead's. Classic style, quite rich and full.
Source: Alness river. VA.

DALWHINNIE
Dalwhinnie, Inverness-shire;
tel: 01528 2208.
Founded 1897. Owned by United Distillers.
Available as 15 year old. Fragrant nose, medium
body, delicious flavour.
Source: Allt an t'Sluic Burn. VW.

DEANSTON
Doune, Stirlingshire.
Constructed 1966 in ancient cotton mill dated
1785. Owned by Burn Stewart. Available as 12,
17 and 21 years old and as 14 and 18 from
Cadenhead's. Light, slightly fruity, smooth.
Source: Teith river. NV.

THE EDRADOUR

Pitlochry, Perthshire PH16 5JP;
tel: 01796 472095.

Founded 1837. Owned by Campbell Distillers. (See **Extremes**, **Smallest**). 100 per cent aged in sherry casks. Available at 10 and 20 years from Cadenhead's. Sherry nose, palate dryish with pleasant finish.

Source: Springs on Mhoulin Moor. VW.

GLEN ALBYN

Inverness.

Founded 1846, demolished 1988. Available 1972 and '73 from Gordon & MacPhail in Connoisseurs Choice and 27 year old from Cadenhead's. Limited nose but quite flavoursome palate.

GLENCADAM

Brechin, Angus, DD9 7PA;
tel: 01356 622217.

Founded c. 1825. Owned by Allied Distillers. Availability very limited, as sherry aged 17 year old from Cadenhead's. Slightly sweet, fullish body.

Source: Moorfoot Loch. VW.

GLEN DEVERON

Macduff Distillery, Banff, Banffshire;
tel: 01261 812612.

Founded 1962. Owned by William Lawson Distillers Ltd. Available as 12 years, some other provision as **Macduff**, for example 14, 16 and 20 year old from Cadenhead's and 1975 from Gordon & MacPhail. Fresh nose, middleweight body, clean finish.

Source: Local springs. VA.

GLEN GARIOCH

Old Meldrum, Aberdeenshire AB5 0ES.
Founded 1798, now mothballed. Owned by
Morrison Bowmore. Available as 1987 bottled at
8, 15 and 21 years. Own maltings.
Source: Spring on Percock Hill.

GLENGOYNE

Dumgoyne, Stirlingshire G63 9LB;
tel: 01360 550254.
Quaint premises founded 1833. Owned by Lang
Bros since 1876. Available at 10, 12 and 17 years
old. (See **Extremes**: **Christmas Day**.) Fresh,
uncomplicated, agreeable, peaks at 17 years.
Source: Waterfall from Campsie Hills. VW.

GLENLOCHY

Fort William, Inverness-shire.
Founded 1898, closed 1983. Available as 1977
from Gordon & MacPhail and in Connoisseurs
Choice and 18 from Cadenhead's. Light but firm,
quite pleasing aroma.
Source: Nevis river.

GLEN MHOR

Inverness.
Founded 1892, demolished 1983. Available as 18
years from Cadenhead's and 8, 12, 1978 and '79
from Gordon & MacPhail and excellent special
bottlings by Unwins of 1969 at 45 per cent.
Slightly aromatic nose, light, gentle, smooth.
Source: Unknown.

GLENMORANGIE

Tain, Ross-shire IV19 1PZ;
tel: 01862 892477.
Founded 1843. Owned by Glenmorangie PLC.

Available as 10 and 18 years Bourbon cask, also 12 year old styles finished in Sherry, Port and Madeira butts. Finishing takes 6–24 months depending on needs. Regular style has delicate floral aroma, clean, well-balanced, quite dry palate.
Source: Tarlogie Springs. VW.

GLEN ORD
Muir of Ord, Ross-shire IV6 7UJ;
tel: 01463 870421.
Founded 1838. Owned by United Distillers. Available as 12 years. Pleasant aroma, middleweight, quite round in mouth.
Source: Allt Fionnaidh. VW.

THE GLENTURRET
Crieff, Perthshire PH7 4HA;
tel: 01764 656565.
Founded 1775, but closed 1923–1959. Owned by The Highland Distilleries Co. PLC. Available as 8, 12, 15, 18, 21 and 25 years, and 1966 from

Gordon & MacPhail and 25 from Cadenhead's.
Medium-flavoured nose, soft attractive mouthful,
long finish.
Source: Loch Turret. VW with excellent facilities.
(See **Extremes**).

GLENUGIE
Peterhead, Aberdeenshire.
Founded 1831, closed 1983. Available as 1966
and '67 in Connoisseurs Choice and 18 years
from Cadenhead's. Fruity nose, pleasant medium
body on palate.
Source: Moors 3–4 miles (4–5 kilometres) away.

GLENURY ROYAL
Stonehaven, Kincardineshire.
Founded 1825, closed 1985. Available as 23 years
from Gordon & MacPhail. Fragrant, slightly smoky
bouquet and palate with light body.
Source: Cowie water.

INCHMURRIN
Loch Lomond Distillery,
Alexandria, Dunbartonshire.
Founded 1965. Owned by Loch Lomond Distillery
Co. Ltd. Available as 9 and 10 year old from
Cadenhead's. Slightly fragrant nose, lightish in
body, easy drinking.
Source: Loch Lomond. VW.

LOCHSIDE
Montrose, Angus.
Founded 1957, now closed. Available as
Connoisseurs Choice 1966 and '81 and as 31
year old single grain from Cadenhead's.
Source: Unknown.

MILBURN

Inverness, Inverness-shire.
Founded 1807, now closed. Available as
Connoisseurs Choice 1972 and 18 years from
Gordon & McPhail. Classic full Highland malt with
dry finish.
Source: Local Sprugs.

NORTH PORT (SOMETIMES CALLED **BRECHIN**)

Brechin, Angus.
Founded 1820, now closed. Available as 1974
from Gordon & MacPhail and 18 years from
Cadenhead's. Light, clean and dry.
Source: Loch Lee.

OBAN

Oban, Argyllshire PA34 5NH;
tel: 01631 62110.
Founded 1794. Owned by United Distillers.
Available in Classic Malt Series as 14 years. Peaty
nose, smooth, fullish.
Source: Loch Gleann and Bhearraidh. VW.

OLD FETTERCAIRN

Fettercairn, Laurencekirk, Kincardineshire;
tel: 01561 340205.
Founded 1824. Owned by Whyte & Mackay.
Available as 10 and 12 years from Cadenhead's.
Classic malty dram with dry finish.
Source: Local springs in Grampians. VW.

OLD PULTENEY (SOMETIMES CALLED **PULTENEY**)

Pulteney Distillery, Wick, Caithness;
tel: 01955 2371.
Founded 1826. Owned by Inver House Distillers.
Available at 8, 12 and 15 years and 1961 from

Gordon & MacPhail. Peaty aroma, some say salty, quite unusual.
Source: Loch of Hempriggs. VW.

RHOSDHU
Loch Lomond Distillery, Alexandria, Dunbartonshire.
The second malt which is produced at this distillery. Owned by Loch Lomond Distillery Co. Ltd. Its sister malt is Inchmurrin.
Source: Loch Lomond. NV.

ROSEBANK
Camelon, Falkirk, Stirlingshire.
Founded 1840, now closed. Available as 12 years in Flora and Fauna series and 1984 Connoisseurs Choice from Gordon & MacPhail. Elegant, light nose, light-medium, very smooth body.
Source: Reservoir in Carron Valley.

ROYAL BRACKLA
Cawdor, Nairnshire;
tel: 016677 404280.
Founded 1812. Owned by United Distillers. Available as 10 years in Flora and Fauna series and 1972 and '74 Connoisseurs Choice. Peaty nose, full body, dry.
Source: Cawdor Burn. VA.

ROYAL LOCHNAGAR
Crathie, Ballater, Aberdeenshire AB3 5TB;
tel: 01339 742273.
Founded 1826. Owned by United Distillers. Available as 12 years and no age for highly priced Select Reserve. Powerful, robust dram, full of flavour.
Source: Lochnagar Springs. VW.

TEANINICH

Alness, Ross-shire;
tel: 01349 882461.
Founded 1817. Owned by United Distillers.
Available at 10 years in Flora and Fauna Series
and 11 year old from Cadenhead's. Smoky,
pleasantly flavoured with good finish.
Source: Dairywell Spring. VA.

TOMATIN

Tomatin, Inverness-shire IV13 7YT;
tel: 01808 511444.
Founded 1897. Owned by Takara Shuzo Co. Ltd
and Okura & Co. Ltd. Available at 10 and 12
years. Slightly peaty, elegant malt.
Source: Allt na Frithe Burn. VW.

TULLIBARDINE

Blackford, Perthshire PH4 1QG.
Founded 1949 on site of orginal Tullibardine
distillery 1798–1837, now mothballed. Owned by
Whyte & Mackay. Available at 10 years. Pleasant,
quite full, easy finish, slightly sweet.
Source: The Danny Burn.

Speyside

ABERLOUR

(-Glenlivet) Aberlour, Banffshire AB38 9PJ;
tel: 01340 871204.
Founded 1826. Owned by Campbell Distillers
(Pernod Ricard group). Available at 10 and 12
years, 15 years (France only), 100 proof non-aged
(duty free), Aberlour Antique non-aged (duty
free) and Vintage, currently 1971 bottled in 1993.
Also 25 year old from Cadenhead's. Classic full-
bodied Speyside, fruity nose, well-rounded body.

Source: St Drostan's Well. VA.

ALLT À BHAINNE

Dufftown, Banffshire.
Founded 1975. Owned by Seagrams. Available as
15 year old from Cadenhead's. NV.

AN CNOC

(-Glenlivet), Knockdhu Distillery, Knock,
Aberdeenshire AB5 5LJ.
A re-naming of Knockdhu originally founded in
1893. Owned by Inver House Distillers. Available
as 12 years. Fragrant aroma, soft, gentle, mellow
dram.
Source: Knock Hill Springs. NV.

AULTMORE

Keith, Banffshire;
tel: 01542 882762.
Founded 1896. Owned by United Distillers. 12
year old available in Flora and Fauna range.
Slightly peaty nose, flavoursome mouthful, good
finish.
Source: Auchinderran Burn. VW.

BALMENACH

(-Glenlivet) Cromdale, Moray.
Founded 1824. Owned by United Distillers and only available in Flora and Fauna series. Aromatic nose, fullish flavour, pleasant.
Source: Cromdale Burn. NV.

THE BALVENIE

(-Glenlivet) Balvenie, Dufftown, Banffshire.
Founded 1892 by W. & J. Grant and still owned by the Grant family as neighbour to Glenfiddich. 10, 12 and 15 year old marketed. Own maltings. Rich bouquet, full flavoured, delicious sweet finish.
Source: Robbie Dubh Burn. NV.

BENRIACH

(-Glenlivet) Longmorn, Elgin, Morayshire IV3 3SJ.
Founded 1898 by Longmorn Distillery Co. Ltd. Owned by Seagram. Own floor maltings. Light nose, middleweight, slightly sweet.
Source: Local springs. NV.

BENRINNES

Aberlour, Banffshire;
tel: 01340 871215.
Founded c. 1826 by Peter McKenzie. Owned by United Distillers. Available as 15 year old in Flora and Fauna series. Fragrant aroma, quite firm, long finish.
Source: Rowantree and Scurran Burns. VA.

BENROMACH

(-Glenlivet) Forres, Morayshire.
Founded 1898, purchased by Gordon & MacPhail in 1993. Now available as 12 year old, also 18 years from Cadenhead's and Scotts Selection 60

per cent 1978. Light fragrant bouquet, elegant, smooth.
Source: Chapeltown Springs. NV.

BRAES OF GLENLIVET
Owned by Seagrams. Available as 8 year old from Cadenhead's. Elegant nose, smooth, agreeable. NV.

CAPERDONICH
Rothes, Morayshire.
Founded 1898. Owned by Seagrams. Available as 1980 and '82 from Gordon & MacPhail and 14 year old from Cadenhead's. Flowery, middleweight, quite smoky.
Source: The Caperdonich Burn. NV.

CARDHU
Knockando, Aberlour, Banffshire IV35 7SB;
tel: 01340 6204
Founded 1824. Owned by United Distillers.
Available as 12 years.
Source: Mannoch Hill and Lyne Burn Springs. VW.

COLEBURN
Longmorn, Elgin, Morayshire.
Founded 1897 by John Robertson & Son Ltd, now mothballed. Owned by United Distillers.
Cadenhead's cask strength 17 year old but generally rare to find.
Source: Glen of Rothes Burn.

CONVALMORE
Dufftown, Banffshire.
Founded 1894 by Convalmore-Glenlivet Distillery Co. Ltd. Owned by United Distillers, now closed.

Available as 17 and 30 year old from Cadenhead's, 1960 and '69 from Gordon & MacPhail.
Source: Springs in the Conval Hills.

CRAGGANMORE
(-Glenlivet) Ballindalloch,
Banffshire AB3 9AB;
tel: 01807 2202.
Founded 1869–70. Owned by United Distillers.
Available as 13 year old from Cadenhead's, 1977 and '78 from Gordon & MacPhail. Dry aroma, firm body, smoky finish.
Source: The Craggan Burn. VA.

CRAIGELLACHIE
(-Glenlivet) Craigellachie, Banffshire.
Founded 1891. Owned by United Distillers.
Limited availability as 14 year old in Flora and Fauna series.
Source: Little Conval Hill. NV.

DAILUAINE

Carron, Morayshire.
Founded 1852. Owned by United Distillers.
Available as 16 year old in Flora and Fauna series.
Source: Bailliemullich Burn. VW.

DRUMGUISH

The Speyside Distillery, Drumguish.
Founded 1990. Owned by the Speyside Distillery
Co. Ltd. Available no age. Mellow dram with a
hint of sweetness.
Source: River Tromie. NV.

DUFFTOWN

(-Glenlivet) Dufftown, Keith, Banffshire;
tel: 01340 820224.
Founded 1896. Owned by United Distillers.
Available as 15 years in Flora and Fauna series.
Source: Jock's Well in the Conval Hills. VA.

GLENBURGIE

(-Glenlivet) Forres, Moray;
tel: 01343 850258.
Founded 1810. Owned by Allied Distillers.
Available at 13, 17 and 28 years old from
Cadenhead's and 8, 1984, '67, '68, '66 and '61
from Gordon & MacPhail and '67 and '68 in
Connoisseurs Choice.
Source: Various local springs. VA.

THE GLENDRONACH

Forgue, Huntly, Aberdeenshire;
tel: 01466 730202.
Founded 1826. Own maltings. Owned by Allied
Distillers. Available at 12 years. Very lightly
peated, smooth round dram.
Source: Springs adjacent to the Dronach Burn. VW.

GLENDULLAN

(-Glenlivet) Dufftown, Keith, Banffshire;
tel: 01340 820250.
Founded 1897. Owned by United Distillers.
Available at 12 years in Flora and Fauna series.
Source: Various springs in the Conval Hills. VW.

GLENFARCLAS

Marypark, Ballindollach, Banffshire;
tel: 01807 500209.
Founded 1836. Independently owned by J & G
Grant. Available at 8 (60 per cent), 10, 12, 15,
21, 25 and 30 years.
Source: Ben Rinnes Springs. VW.

GLENFIDDICH

(-Glenlivet) Dufftown, Keith, Banffshire;
tel: 01340 820373.
Founded 1886. Owned by Wm Grant & Sons Ltd.
Available with no age given.
*No 1 selling malt in the world.
Source: Robbie Dubh Spring. VW.

GLENGLASSAUGH

Portsoy, Banffshire AB45 2SQ;
tel: 01261 42367.
Founded 1875, now mothballed. Owned by The
Highland Distilleries Co. PLC. Available at 12
years. Delicate nose, slightly sweet finish.
Source: The Glassaugh Spring.

GLEN GRANT

(-Glenlivet) Rothes, Moray AB38 7BS;
tel: 01542 783318.
Founded 1840. Owned by Seagrams. Available at
no age, 5 and 10 years.
Source: Caperdonich Well. VW.

GLEN KEITH

(-Glenlivet) Keith, Banffshire;
tel: 01542 783042.
Founded 1957. Owned by Seagrams. Available in
Connoisseurs Choice as 1983.
Source: Balloch Hill Springs. VA.

THE GLENLIVET

Ballindalloch, Banffshire AB3 9DB;
tel: 01542 783220.
Founded 1824. (See **First or Oldest**). Owned by
Seagrams. Available at 12, 18 and 21 years and at
25 from Gordon & MacPhail. Fine bouquet, gentle
palate, some sweetness. Source: Josie's Well. VW.

GLENLOSSIE

(-Glenlivet) Birnie, Elgin, Morayshire;
tel: 01343 86331.
Founded 1876. Owned by United Distillers.
Available in Flora and Fauna series at 10 years.
Aromatic nose, smooth palate.
Source: Bardon Burn. VW.

GLEN MORAY

Elgin, Moray IV30 1YE;
tel: 01343 542577.
Founded 1897. Owned by MacDonald & Muir.
Available as 12 and 15 years. Gentle bouquet,
smooth finish.
Source: Lossie River. VW.

THE GLENROTHES

Rothes, Moray.
Founded 1878. Owned by Highland Distilleries
Company Ltd. Distributed by Berry, Bros. & Rudd.
Available as 12 years. Light bouquet, smooth,
fullish.
Source: Glenrothes Springs. NV.

GLEN SPEY

Rothes, Moray.
Founded c. 1878. Owned by IDV (Grand
Metropolitan Group). Available as 15 year old
from Cadenhead's.
Source: The Doonie Burn. NV.

GLENTAUCHERS

(-Glenlivet) Mulben, Banffshire;
tel: 01542 860272.
Founded 1898. Owned by Allied Distillers.
Available as 1979 from Gordon & MacPhail.
Unusual sweetish nose, yet dry finish.
Source: Mulben Springs. VA.

IMPERIAL

(-Glenlivet) Carron, Moray AB38 7QP;
tel: 01340 810276.
Founded 1897. Owned by Allied Distillers.

Available as 1979 from Gordon & MacPhail.
Smoky bouquet, mellow, fullish flavour.
Source: Ballintomb Burn. VA.

INCHGOWER
Buckie, Banffshire;
tel: 01542 831161.
Founded 1872. Owned by United Distillers.
Available as 14 years in Flora and Fauna series.
Slightly sweet, attractive flavour.
Source: Menduff Springs. VW.

KININVIE
(-Glenlivet) Dufftown, Keith, Banffshire.
Owned by Wm Grant Ltd of Glenfiddich fame.
Founded 1990. No malt yet available. NV.

KNOCKANDO

Knockando, Moray;
tel: 01340 6205.

Founded 1898. Owned by IDV. Available under excellent method where distillery manager selects malt of the season at peak age. For examples, distilled 1984, bottled in 1997. Also 1970 and '80 from Gordon & MacPhail and 12 year old from Cadenhead's. Pleasant aroma, middleweight, mellow flavour.
Source: Cardnach Spring. VA.

LINKWOOD

Elgin, Moray;
tel: 01343 547004.

Founded 1820. Owned by United Distillers. Available as 12 years. Light smokiness, slightly sweet, mellow.
Source: Milbuies Loch. VA.

LONGMORN

(-Glenlivet) Elgin, Moray.

Founded 1894. Owned by Seagrams. Available as 12 and 15 years, also 1962 and '69 from Gordon & MacPhail. Fragrant aroma, full-bodied, slightly sweet.
Source: Boreholes. NV.

THE MACALLAN

(-Glenlivet) Craigellachie, Banffshire;
tel: 01340 871471.

Founded 1824. Owned by Highland Distillers Co. PLC. Available as 7, 10, 12, 18, 25 and 1976/77 from Gordon & MacPhail. Prominent sherry nose, very smooth, good finish.
Source: Boreholes. VA.

MANNOCHMORE

near Elgin, Moray.

Founded 1971. Owned by United Distillers.

Available as 1984 from Gordon & MacPhail. Light aroma, quite smooth.

Source: The Bardon Burn. NV.

MILTONDUFF

Elgin, Moray IV30 3TQ;

tel: 01343 547433.

Founded 1824. Owned by Allied Distillers.

Available as 12 years. Fragrant nose, smooth, middleweight.

Source: Loch Moray. VA.

MOSSTOWIE

(-Glenlivet)

(second operation at Milton Duff 1964–81).

Available as 1975 and '79 from Gordon & MacPhail. Pleasant nose, smooth, good finish.

Source: Loch Moray.

MORTLACH

Dufftown, Banffshire;
tel: 01840 820318.
Founded 1924. Owned by United Distillers.
Available as 16 years in Flora and Fauna series
and 15, 21, 1961 and '66 from Gordon & McPhail.
Mellow bouquet, smooth, beautifully balanced.
Source: Conval Hill Springs. VA.

PITTYVAICH

(-Glenlivet) Dufftown Keith, Banffshire, (now
closed).
Owned by United Distillers. Available as 12 years
in Flora and Fauna series. Fine bouquet, mellow,
fullish flavour.
Source: Convalleys and Balliemore Springs.

THE SINGLETON OF AUCHROISK

Mulben, Banffshire AB55 3XS;
tel: 01542 860633.
Founded 1974. Owned by IDV. Available as 10 and
12 years and 10 from Gordon & MacPhail and 12
from Cadenhead's. Rich, smooth, full-bodied
dram.
Source: Dorie's Well (See **Extremes**). VA.

STRATHISLA

(-Glenlivet) Keith, Banffshire AB55 3BS;
tel: 01542 783044.
Founded 1786. Owned by Seagrams. Available as
12 years and 21 years, 1960, '63, '67, and '80
and '72, also '54. Fragrant aroma, slightly sweet,
good finish.
Source: Fons Bulliens Well. VW.

SPEYBURN

(-Glenlivet) Rothes, Moray IV33 7AG.
Founded 1897. Owned by Inver House Distillers.
Available as 10 and 21 years and 1971 in
Connoisseurs Choice. Slightly honeyed nose, well-
balanced palate, dry finish.
Source: The Granty Burn. VA.

STRATHMILL

(-Glenlivet)
Founded 1891. Owned by IDV. Generally used only
for blending. Available as 11 year old from
Cadenhead's.
Source: Local wells. NV.

TAMDHU

(-Glenlivet) Knockando, Aberlour, Banffshire
IV35 7RR;
tel: 013406 221.
Founded 1896. Owned by Matthew Gloag & Son.
Available no age and 16, 29 and 30 years old
from Cadenhead's. Own Maltings. Gentle
bouquet, slightly sweet, mellow.
Source: Tamdhu Spring. VW.

TAMNAVULIN

(-Glenlivet) Ballindalloch, Banffshire, (now
mothballed).
Founded 1965. Owned by Whyte & Mackay.
Available as 10 years, also Stillman's Dram at 25
years, 12 from Gordon & MacPhail and 25 from
Cadenhead's. Lightish nose, slightly sweet palate.
Source: Natural underground reservoir. VW.

TOMINTOUL

(-Glenlivet) Ballindalloch.
Founded 1964. Owned by Whyte & Mackay.
Available as 10 years. Fine bouquet, gentle
palate.
Source: Ballantruan Spring. NV.

THE TORMORE

Advie, Grantown-on-Spey, Moray;
tel: 01807 510244.
Founded 1959. Owned by Allied Distillers.
Available as 10 years. Slightly aromatic nose,
middleweight, slightly sweet.
Source: Achvochkie Burn. VW.

Other Whisky-Producing Countries

Whisky has been, and still is, produced in more countries than are generally acknowledged. A substantial proportion is made by blending local distilled spirit with imported Scotch whisky, but a surprising number of countries make their own malts.

world-wide   There appear to be around 40 countries throughout the world which have made their own whiskies at some time and no doubt there are others that are not listed.

Argentina   The best-known of several whiskies is the Seagram-owned San Ignacio from Tucuman, 1000 miles (1600 kilometres) north of Buenos Aires.

Austria   A small specialist distiller, Franz Böckl, produces 3 pot-still whiskies in Deutsch-Wagram; Austrian Rye, Austrian Oats and Austrian Barley. Several own-label blends use imported Scotch single malt as a base.

Australia   There is no longer an active whisky distillery, but Australia has had several in the past including Myer's Ballarat, Corio, Chessboard, Marksman and Gilbey's.

Bolivia   It is reported that D&B, Tommy Lonsdale and Cutter are made, based on Scotch malt whisky; also one or two Bourbon styles.

Brazil   Blended whiskies include Drury's and Old Eight.

Bulgaria   Some Seagram and Suntory brands are distilled under licence.

Costa Rica   A distillery is owned by Seagrams.

Croatia   Now here is a riddle. The only known Croatian whisky was correctly labelled as Luxardo Italian whisky during its sole period of production, between 1936 and 1938, at Zara in Dalmatia. Few people other than patriotic Italians and students of Balkan history will be aware that an Italian enclave occupied the region under the Austro-Hungarian Empire from 1867 to 1918, and then as part of Italy from 1919 to 1947.

Whisky was produced in Croatia because of territorial disputes and politics elsewhere. The League of Nations had imposed commercial sanctions on Italy because of its invasion of Ethiopia. Luxardo, situated in Zara and famed for Maraschino, imported Scotch whisky but the company suddenly found its supplies withdrawn and subsequently made the only whisky ever produced in the region.

Czech Republic   Some own-label blended whiskies are produced.

Denmark   In the mid-twentieth century Cloc, Red Lion, Special Wonder, Straight Label and Hamlet brands were available.

Egypt   In 1951 Sir Robert Bruce Lockart wrote of an Egyptian whisky called Bolonacht.

Finland   Lion Blend is reported to be a blend of Scotch malt and Finnish grain spirit.

France   The William Pitters company, near Bordeaux, produces some blends for supermarket sales.

Germany   Racke Rauchzart is a successful whisky.

Guyana   Some blended whiskies are reported.

India   Growing rapidly as a whisky-producing nation, India has major distilleries in Amriza, Bangalore, Bombay and near Delhi. Bagpiper is the top-selling label, with just over 50 million bottles in 1996.

Iran   There were at least three blended whiskies before the rise of the Ayatollah Khomeni.

Italy   See Croatia.

Japan   Though not as large as it was, Japan is a major producer. Suntory Kakubin is the top brand and Suntory own all five leading Japanese whiskies.

Korea   A few blends are available; Something Special is a popular brand.

Mexico   There are distilleries for both Seagrams and Suntory brands.

Netherlands   Bols Gold Top whisky was first distilled in 1933 but ceased around 1980.

New Zealand   Unlicensed whisky production began with the arrival of Scottish immigrants on South Island in 1848. By 1873 The New Zealand Distillery in Dunedin, run by Howden and Robertson, had a capacity of nearly 450,000 litres (100,000 gallons) a year. Today Wilsons, a six-year-old blend of a Scotch style, is produced by Seagrams at Dunedin, as is Lammerlaw, a 10-year-old single malt which draws its water from the Lammerlaw hills. In the past they have made a Bourbon style called 45 South.

Norway   Some years ago a brand called Club Blend was marketed, but it is no longer available.

Peru   Quite a busy whisky country, Peru has seven distilleries, five of which make Scotch-style whiskies and two Bourbon types.

The Phillipines   A small volume of own-label blended whisky is produced.

Russia A brand called Pollynnaia is distilled and blended near Odessa.

Singapore There are unconfirmed rumours of a blended whisky called Johnnie Talker.

South Africa Vatted malts and blends produced in the country make up around 12 per cent of all whiskies sold there. Three Ships, launched in 1977, is the leader. Knights and Teals are also successful.

Spain An active producer, Spain's leading brand is Whisky DYC (owned by Allied Domecq).

Switzerland Three blends are made including one by Pernod.

Tanzania A Zanzibar whisky made by Gilbeys.

Thailand A blend called Red Cock.

Uruguay There are several brands with distinctively Scottish-sounding names like Spey Royal and MacDougall.

Venezuela The La Miel distillery, 400 kilometres (250 miles) west of Caracas, makes a whisky.

Zambia A blend made by Gilbeys.

Intriguing Stories

Alte Kornschnapps   Believe it or not, this was the name given to the first whisky produced in Seagram's history. Joseph Seagram had not joined his future employers, Hespeler, Randall and Roos, when in 1857 they began selling Alte Kornschnapps from barrels in their King Street, Waterloo shop in Ontario. Seagram later became outright owner of the business. The curious name was chosen because the town had been settled by five hundred Germans.

a fairlie long time   The phrase might best describe the time spent building the Speyside distillery at Drumguish in Scotland. In 1970 its founder George Christie, a keen advocate of traditional skills, hired Alex Fairlie to hand-build the entire property in truly rustic style. Alex is a stone-dyker, an old-fashioned Scottish craftsman. He preferred to work alone and knew that the task would take many years. George, one of the few independent whisky producers, realised that a similar period of time is necessary to craft the finest malts and so was prepared to be patient. But even he must sometimes have wondered about a completion date. Finally, in 1990, Alex applied the final touches to a new building that already looked about two hundred years old. George was happy; he had purchased the land in 1956 and craftsmanship was worth the wait. In any case he still had to make his first whisky in the new distillery and that would certainly take another ten or more years – long enough, perhaps, for Alex to build half a warehouse.

most unusual bilingual whisky labels   Te Bheag (pronounced 'chey vek') translates as 'the little lady' and Poit Dhubh (pronounced 'potch ghoo') means 'the black pot'. These are two Gaelic-language labelled whiskies produced by Pràban Na Linne who are based on Skye off the west coast of Scotland. A few years ago they found some unexpected fans in Canada when fifth generation Gaelic-speaking islanders on Cape Breton, Nova Scotia, began placing orders. However, when the company made inquiries with the Canadian government about exporting, it was shocked to learn that a bilingual English and French label would be required. The regulation was overruled by the Nova Scotia Liquor

Commission who authorised the only Gaelic–French labels on earth.

Peter Scott   This brand is produced by Khoday's distillery, Bangalore, India. In the mid-1960s Peter Warren, the distillery manager at the Ben Nevis distillery in the Highlands of Scotland, accepted the role of building and developing this new distillery in India. He invited his son, also Peter, to join him and they soon created a new three-year-old Indian whisky blend with a suitable name.

Tullamore Dew   One of the great names of Irish whiskey, it flourished in the latter part of the nineteenth century. Its general manager, Daniel E. Williams, became part-owner and quickly renamed the most popular style as Tullamore Dew, simply by using his three initials. He then introduced an advertising slogan: Give every man his Dew.

bring on the artillery   Determination was certainly a characteristic of John Downes, an eighteenth-century excise man based in Limerick, who was not prepared to admit defeat. On 20 February 1788, having been regularly frustrated by his inability to gain access to a known illicit distillery within the fortified walls of the castle of Ognally, he summoned military help. This duly arrived in the form of a detachment of the 27th regiment, who placed two artillery guns in front of the castle and threatened to bombard it. The residents, aware that any fire could blow them all to smithereens, quickly decided to surrender Ireland's largest-ever unofficial distillery.

wartime whisky   There are many reports that during the Second World War Scotch whisky distilleries were commandeered by the British government for industrial purposes, but this was not always the case.

Production continued at the now defunct distillery with the most thrilling address in Scotland – the Banff Distillery, Mill of Banff, Banff, Banffshire. The reason why misguided Luftwaffe pilots strafed and bombed the distillery will probably never be known. However, their actions produced chaos among the local animal population. To avoid the risk of explosion and of fire spreading, some of the warehouse stocks were jettisoned and ran away into surrounding ditches and streams where they were consumed by birds and farm animals. This resulted in cows that could not stand up to be milked and a dawn chorus sung out-of-tune at midday.

A few miles west of Glasgow the Auchentoshan distillery was a somewhat unfortunate victim. Indeed, visitors today can see two flat-roofed houses that once had peaks. Its site at Old Kilpatrick is just downstream from the shipbuilding yards of Clydebank, a brave town where only seven properties escaped serious damage. By chance Auchentoshan stood near two oil depots of vital importance and to protect them two large round decoy tanks were built on either side of the distillery. This ingenious ploy proved successful one sad day when a German plane succeeded in bombing along a straight line between them, destroying an ageing warehouse and removing the tops from two staff houses.

the Queen's rusty old barrel   The Bowmore distillery on Islay is enjoying a golden era. Not only is it winning medals, but it has also been awarded the privilege of keeping Her Majesty the Queen's only barrel of single malt. It rests inside Bowmore's legendary warehouse where the high tide sweeps halfway up the wall twice every day and permeates the building with a salty sea tangle. Inside, the royal cask like all the others, displays rungs that are pitted with rust. As the whisky evaporates, losing 2 per cent per annum, the lost atmosphere is replaced by the briny breath of the salt-watered Lochindaal. The result is an iodine aroma that balances superbly with the peaty undertones of a magnificent malt.

love or hate   Iain Henderson, the amiable manager of the Laphroaig distillery on Islay, is not one to mince his words. He believes that Laphroaig is one of – if not the most – pungent, aromatic and full-flavoured whiskies in the world, and accepts that it is not for fence-sitters. 'Yer weel eithur luv it or hayt it', he has been heard to say on many occasions, 'but dee at leest tree it once.' Even he might have been a trifle taken aback by the performance of Lesley Williams, a respected television news journalist who was taping a special feature for BAY-TV in San Francisco. The location was the Ritz-Carlton's record-breaking malt whisky bar, an innovation in that city's life-style. Unaware of the differing characteristics of single malts, she insisted upon picking one at random and drinking it to conclude the filming. She stepped forward, seized a large Laphroaig, swallowed, pulled a horrified face and did the unmentionable.

the luck of the Irish   In the rugged north-west of Ireland the inhabitants still talk about their ancient kingdom of Tyrconnell, once ruled by the mighty O'Donnells. In the latter part of the nineteenth century, Londonderry distiller Andrew Watt shipped the first Tyrconnell pot still whiskey across the Atlantic with some success.

Its name arose because in 1876 the Watt family's racehorse, Tyrconnell, a rank outsider but supported by many employees, won what was then the only Irish classic – the Queen Victoria Plate – at the remarkable odds of 100 to 1. The celebrations were extraordinary and afterwards to record the occasion, the Watt company created a colourful label showing its horse heading for the line. The 1992 restoration of Tyrconnell single malt Irish whiskey by the Cooley distillery has seen the colourful label back in service.

whisky for the Eucharist   Two reports exist of whisky being used for the Eucharist. The first was before the battle of Culloden in 1746 when oatcake and whisky were blessed and taken. One account tells how a Scottish priest, preparing to give communion to some of Bonnie Prince Charlie's soldiers, found himself without the sacred host or consecrated wine and so made use of what was available. Another report of the battle records that the same Eucharist was given to a dying clan leader during his last rites.

Whisky in Literature and Song

American Journal of Sociology, July 1901

Three drinks of mountain dew cause on average one fight.

American Pie (Don McLean, 1972)

So, bye, bye, Miss American Pie
Drove my Chevy to the levee
But the levee was dry
Them good old boys was drinkin'
Whiskey and rye
Singin' this'll be the day that I die.

Anonymously written popular Scottish song:

Campbeltown Loch I wish you were whisky,
Campbeltown Loch, Och Aye!
Campbeltown Loch I wish you were whisky,
I would drink you dry.

Sam Bronfman

The man largely responsible for the Seagram dynasty would not have made many claims to literary merit but his succinct comment on distilling sums up the basic truth about whisky production:

Distilling is a science, blending is an art.

Robert Burns

The legendary Scottish poet, wrote of Lowland whisky:

a most rascally liquor: and by consequence only drank by the most rascally part of the inhabitants.

At the time many Lowland distillers were using rye and wheat and no doubt Burns found this inferior to barley.

In 'Auld Lang Syne.': he wrote

We'll tak' a cup of kindness yet, for Auld Lang Syne.

in Burns' poem 'Scotch Drink':

O Whisky! soul a' plays an' pranks!
Accept a Bardie's grateful thanks!
When wanting thee, what tuneless cranks
Are my poor verses!

Derek Cooper

The resonant voice and reasoning hand of whisky-writers, wrote in 1989 of an old Highland saying:

One whisky is alright;
Two is too much;
three is too few.

James Feehan

Nineteenth-century Irish poet in praise of Coleraine whisky:

The Spaniard may boast of his shadow
The Frenchman his sparkling Champagne
But if a man wants to be merry
I'd advise him to try Ould Coleraine.

John Heath-Stubbs

'A Charm Against the Toothache' (1954)

Venerable Mother Toothache
Climb down from the white battlements
Stop twisting in your yellow fingers
The fourfold rope of nerves;
And tomorrow I'll give you a tot of whisky
To hold in your cupped hands,
A garland of anise flowers
and three cloves like nails.

Raphael Holinshed

In his *Chronicles of England, Scotland and Ireland* (1578) wrote of *uisge beatha*:

Beying moderatelie taken, it sloweth age, it strengtheneth youthe: it helpeth digestion; it cutteth fleume; it abandoneth melancholie; it relisheth the harte; it lighteneth the mynde; it quickeneth the spirites; it cureth the hydropsie; it healeth the strangury [difficulty in urinating]; it pounceth the stone. It repelleth gravel; it puffeth away ventosite.

Dr Samuel Johnson

In his *Journey to the Western Isles of Scotland*, written in 1775, made surprisingly few references to the drink. Yet perhaps that was not surprising; despite being a great man of letters and famed gourmand, he was not a noted gourmet and his addition of lumps of sugar to both lemonade and port hints at why *usquebaugh* was not a priority on his list of drinks. He was, though, an astute observer of his fellow men. At an inn at Anoch in Glenmorrison, in the Highlands, following a busy evening session:

they were joined by some soldiers who had great indignation at the bad qualities of usquebaugh.

Upon describing the life-style of a typical Hebridean:

No man is so abstemious as to refuse the morning dram, which they call a skalk.

(This was served before breakfast.)

When defining usquebaugh:

The word 'usquebaugh' means water, and is applied by way of eminence to strong water, or distilled liquor. The spirit drunk in the North is drawn from barley. I never tasted it, except once for experiment at the inn in Inverary, when I thought it preferable to any English malt brandy [another term for English whisky]. It was

strong, but not pungent, and was free from
the empyreumatic taste or smell.

James Joyce
The light music of whiskey falling into a glass –
an agreeable interlude.

Compton Mackenzie
The prolific author spent the Second World War
on the Hebridean island of Barra, and by chance
witnessed a dramatic incident which he made use
of in a 1946 novel and 1947 film. *Whisky Galore*
was based on the real-life shipwreck of the
Politician on the rocks of the neighbouring isle of
Ericksay. Its cargo of thousands of cases of Scotch
whisky were retrieved by the islanders, who in turn
were hunted by the excise men.

F. Marian McNeill
In *The Scots Cellar* (1956):

> There are two things a Highlander likes naked
> and one of them is malt whisky.

The writer was clearly incorrect. Every Highland
distiller appears to prefer a malt dressed with a
little spring water which stimulates its bouquet,

arouses its aroma and adds to the pleasure gained from its consumption.

John Marston (1604)

The Dutchman for a drunkard
The Dane for golden locks
The Irishman for *uisca beatha*
The Frenchman for the pox.

John L. O'Sullivan

(Not the American pugilist but an editor) is credited with the following comment on whiskey:

A torchlight procession marching down your throat.

His favourite brand was unknown!

Sir Walter Scott

Wrote in an epitaph to his beloved servant Tom Purdie:

Here lies one who might be trusted with untold gold, but not with unmeasured whisky.

Mark Twain

Life on the Mississippi (1833)

Give an Irishman lager for a month and he's a dead man. An Irishman is lined with copper and the beer corrodes it. But whiskey polishes the copper and is the saving of him.

Whisky Museums

The Oscar Getz American Whiskey Museum

Spalding Hall, 114 N Fifth Street, Bardstown, Kentucky 40004, USA;

tel: 502 348 2999

Open May–October every day except Sunday a.m.; November–April. Tuesday–Sunday.

A fascinating museum with very well-informed staff. It is the centre for the annual Kentucky Bourbon Festival, normally held in the third week of September, which provides a most entertaining final weekend including the 'world barrel rolling championships, the great Kentucky Bourbon tasting and gala dinner dance'. Situated in delightful Bardstown, the extremely friendly capital of Kentucky Bourbon.

The Seagram Museum

57 Erb Street West, Waterloo, Ontario N2L 6C2, Canada;
tel: 519 885 1857; fax: 519 746 1673
Open May–December 10 a.m. – 6 p.m. every day; January–April 10 a.m. – 6 p.m. Tuesday–Sunday.
Spacious, informative exhibition of artefacts and equipment covering whiskies from Canada, the United States and Scotland. A new research project on the life of Joseph Emms Seagram is being prepared.

The Scotch Whisky Heritage Centre

354 Castlehill, The Royal Mile, Edinburgh EH1 2NE (at the entrance to Edinburgh Castle);
tel: 0131 220 0441; fax: 0131 220 6288
Open 10 a.m. – 5.30 p.m. every day. Some extended hours in summer.
Unbelievably open on New Year's Day.
An ideal start to any whisky trip to Scotland. An informative balance of audio-visuals, holistics and a ride back through the centuries with a commentary in eight different languages.

Whisky Specialists

The Athanaeum, Piccadilly, London Bar with nearly a hundred malts available by the glass.

Wm Cadenhead Three retail shops:
Cadenhead Whisky Shop, 172 Canongate, Edinburgh EH8 8BN;
tel: 0131 556 5864; fax: 0131 556 2527
Eaglesome of Campbeltown, Reform Square, Campbeltown, Argyll;
tel: 01586 551710; fax: 01586 553232
Covent Garden Whisky Shop, 3 Russell Street, London WC2B 5JD;
tel: 0171 379 4640; fax: 0171 379 4600
All three shops offer a wide range of old and rare Scotch malts. The London shop also has a good selection of Irish whiskeys.

Gordon & MacPhail
George House, Boroughbriggs Road, Elgin, Moray IV30 1JY;
tel: 01343 545111; fax: 01343 540155
World's largest whisky merchants specialise in rare and old Scotch malts and a few Irish whiskeys with truly remarkable stocks and outstanding international service.

The Malt Whisky Collection at the Ritz-Carlton San Francisco
600 Stockton at California Street, San Francisco, USA;
tel: 415 296 7465; fax: 415 291 0288
Extraordinary offering of around 125 single malt Scotch whiskies.

Master of Malt

96A Calverly Road, Tunbridge Wells, Kent
TN1 2UN;
tel: 01892 750415; fax: 01892 750487
Wide range of regular and special bottlings.

Milroy's

3 Greek Street, Soho, London W1V 6NX;
tel: 0171 437 0893 / 2385; fax: 0171 437 1345
A fascinating variety of malts and blends, always
has something curious on sale. Stock includes a
few unique Milroy own bottlings, notably Milroy's
Glenlivet Sherrywood 16 year old and Milroy's
Craigellachie 1982. Also a wide range of Scotch
malts and blends and 22 different Irish whiskeys.

Murray McDavid

56 Walton Street, Knightsbridge, London
SW3 1RB;
tel: 0171 584 9855; fax: 0171 581 0250
Range of six vintage Scotch single malts.

The Scotch Malt Whisky Society

The Vaults, 87 Giles Street, Leith, Edinburgh
EH6 6BZ;
tel: 0131 555 2266; fax: 0131 553 1003
Members-only society, with historic premises; buys
young spirit and mature Scotch single malts from
distillers for own restricted bottlings, always sold
at cask strength. Sends regular lists and
newsletters.

Scott's Selection, the Speyside Distillery Co. Ltd

Duchess Road, Rutherglen, Glasgow G73 1AU;
tel: 01245 380573; fax: 01245 381232
Small but interesting variety of mature Scotch
single malts at cask strength, chosen by veteran
taster Bob Scott.

Signatory Vintage Scotch Whisky Co. Ltd

7–8 Elizafield, Newhaven Road, Edinburgh
EH6 5PY;
tel: 0131 555 4988; fax: 0131 555 5211
Mostly single cask bottlings. Specialist range of
Silent Stills from closed Scotch single malt
distilleries.

The Whisky Shop

87 Bailgate, Lincoln LN1 3AR;
tel: 01522 537834; fax: 01522 512863
Charming small shop just below the imposing
edifice of Lincoln Cathedral. Offers wide variety
of Irish and Scotch whiskies with around 400
different labels, including a fine selection of
special decanters and limited bottlings.

Whiskyspeak

aqua vitae   The old Latin term for spirits. It was widely used to identify whisky before the arrival of licensed distilling.

Bourbon casks   Charred oak barrels are used for the ageing of Bourbon. Many are sold afterwards to the Scotch whisky industry for re-use, when the effect of the charring has been dulled.

burnt ale   Sometimes called 'pot ale', or 'spent wash', it is the residue after first distillation and is often processed into animal feed.

cask strength   Implies that a whisky has been bottled without being diluted. That is, it is around 57–60 per cent alcohol by volume rather than approximately 40–43 per cent.

chill-filtering   A refrigeration process that clarifies whiskies. It is sometimes omitted by specialist bottlers.

Coffey still   The patent still, registered by Aeneas Coffey in 1830, which produces grain spirit.

column still   A North American continuous still. It is used for all but the few pot-still whiskies.

de-luxe scotch whisky   A blend with a higher proportion of malts and a greater age than premium brands. Many are 12 years old or more.

diastase   An enzyme developed through germination which enables starch to convert to maltose sugar. This in turn produces alcohol.

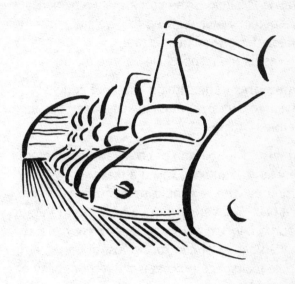

feints (sometimes called tails)   The impure spirit which is the last section of the distillation.

foreshots (sometimes called heads)   The impure spirit that is the first section of the distillation.

grain whisky   Made in Scotland from maize, wheat or barley using a Coffey (continuous) still. It is somewhat lighter than malt whisky with which it is blended to provide Scotch blended whisky.

grist mill   Any size mill that grinds cereals into grist, making it suitable for using in a mash.

hogshead   Cask with a volume of 250 litres (55 gallons).

low wines   The result of the first distillation of the wash. These are then re-distilled to produce the spirit which, when aged, can be called whisky.

malt   Malting is the process whereby barley is steeped in water, allowed to germinate and then dried. The germination creates maltose sugar. The process is the responsibility of the maltman.

marrying   The settling and brief additional ageing of whiskies that have just been blended before bottling.

mash   The solution of cereal and hot water in a very large container, called a mash tun, which produces *wort*, a curious name for what in effect is a beer. The cereals can be mixed as in Kentucky Bourbon, which always includes corn, rye and malted barley, or can consist just of barley, as in single malts. The process is the responsibility of the mashman.

middle cut (sometimes called the heart)   The pure spirit which is the central part of the distillation and which will be the future whisky.

moonshine   Normally indicates illicit whiskey, usually made at night, out of doors, in densely wooded areas of North America. Moonshine still exists in certain country regions with poor economies. It was, of course, a result of the introduction of whiskey taxes two centuries ago and some people just like to maintain old traditions.

The 1901 *American Journal of Sociology* in an article entitled 'Kentucky Mountains and their

Feuds' observed the financial necessity for moonshine at that time: 'Corn, rye and apples find a market when made into moonshine whiskey, while there would be no demand for them as corn, rye and apples.'

mothballed   A military term adopted by the whisky industry. It indicates that the operation of a distillery has been placed temporarily in abeyance with the hope of being restored to production later.

patent still   Similar, or even the same, as Coffey still or column still.

peat   Decomposed vegetable matter before it is carbonised. It influences water sources for some malt whiskies where the barley is steeped in the peaty water. It is also cut and dried in blocks and then burnt to smoke, or peat, the barley following germination; the smoke is called 'peatreek'. This imparts phenols which give a peaty, or phenolic, bouquet to the whisky.

peedie minster   A cask filled with young spirit and presented annually to a local clergyman by the Highland Park distillery on Orkney. It is a tradition which might mistakenly be seen as a form of bribery but in fact is what some modern marketing folk call an educational tool. Its purpose is to dissuade the recipient from supporting any misguided movement in favour of total abstinence or prohibition. It has a 100 per cent success rate.

pot still   The classic copper still that is used for producing malt whiskies in Scotland, Ireland, New

Zealand, the United States and elsewhere, also for Irish whiskey made from a blend of malted and unmalted barley.

rectification   The process of refining a spirit by repeated distillation.

run   The flow of raw spirit which results from distillation.

shebeen   A poor, unlicensed bar where illicit spirits could be consumed. Shebeens were in use in the eighteenth and nineteenth centuries in Ireland and Scotland and some possibly still exist today.

single malt   A whisky that is produced from 100 per cent malted barley in one distillery.

source   See **Water source**: **Did You Know**?

spirit safe   The metal and glass apparatus through which all the second distillation runs, and where the distiller or stillman decides when to take the middle cut, or heart. Upon being collected this is called the spirit.

stillman The person responsible for operating the actual still, rather than other processes in whisky production. He decides at what point to start taking the middle cut.

straight whiskey A term used in North America since the late nineteenth century to make the point that, unlike Scotch blended whisky, it is not blended with grain spirit.

trestarig An ancient Gaelic term meaning triple-distilled.

uisge baoghal An ancient Gaelic term for quadruple distillation. This was an occasional practice in the Western Isles of Scotland in an attempt to lighten heavy whiskies.

underback The vessel which receives the wort from the mash tun.

vatted malts A blend of different single malts. Glenforres from Campbell Distillers is an excellent example.

wash A clear solution, with an alcohol level of around 7–8 per cent, which is the result of fermenting wort.

washback The large vessel in which the wash ferments.

whisky In general it is a spirit that has been distilled from one or more of certain cereals and then aged in oak. There are different legal definitions in various countries.

worm A coiled copper tube of decreasing diameter that acts as a condenser. It is attached to a pot still and kept cold with continuous running water.

wort The sweet solution, or un-fermented beer, that is the result of the mash. It is fermented in a washback, or fermenter, and produces wash.

Can You Remember?

1   The temperature of the coldest source for a Scotch single malt distillery?

2   The name of New Zealand's only single malt whisky?

3   Who looked 'like King Edward VII'?

4   The total abstainer who became the first woman distillery owner in Scotland?

5   The top-selling Indian whisky?

6   The 'Whisky Italiano' that was made in what is now Croatia?

7   The location of the first whisky distillery in Australia?

8   What is the 'leeching process'?

9   What Yack Yack was?

10   Jim Beam's middle name?

11   The foundation date of the first whisky distillery in America?

12   The whiskey that flowed in Marconi's veins?

13   The premium Scotch blend that resulted from the love affair of two Italians?

14   The country in which Three Ships is the leading national whisky brand?

15   Who Lanty Slee was?

16   How many bottles the smallest distillery in Scotland releases each year?

17 The owner of the first major whisky distillery in Canada?

18 The number of whiskies in the Ultimate blend?

19 The founder of the first commercial whiskey distillery in Kentucky?

20 Whose first whisky was called Alte Kornschnapps?

The answers can be found on the following pages:

1: page 1; **2**: page 124; **3**: 21; **4**: 25; **5**: 123; **6**: 122; **7**: 8; **8**: 11; **9**: 58; **10**: 10; **11**: 8; **12**: 40; **13**: 15–16; **14**: 125; **15**: 67; **16**: 6; **17**: 36; **18**: 6; **19**: 8; **20**: 126.